The Cornerstones of
Engaging Leadership

Marta —
Best wishes as
you engage!

D1404544

■ ■ ■ ■ ■ ■ ■ ■ ■ ■

Praise for *The Cornerstones of Engaging Leadership*

"Anyone striving to increase engagement will find this book to be extremely practical and useful. By spelling out a simple, yet powerful, approach to engaging others, this excellent book gives leaders the tools they need to build trust and increase engagement."

STEPHEN M. R. COVEY, AUTHOR OF THE SPEED OF TRUST

"Through sound principles, relevant examples, and a robust set of tools, Casey Wilson helps leaders better understand engagement and the critical role they play in cultivating higher levels of trust, engagement, and ultimately performance . . . an invaluable resource for anyone in a leadership position."

STEPHEN B. KING, CHIEF LEARNING OFFICER, CONSTELLATION ENERGY

"A fine balance of theory and practice, Casey Wilson's The Cornerstones of Engaging Leadership *takes a fresh look at what really matters most to good leaders . . . getting workers excited about what they do!"*

COLONEL DAVID B. FILIPPI, UNITED STATES AIR FORCE (RET)

"Finally! A book that successfully illustrates how real investment in an organization's most precious resource— people—can positively impact the bottom line and create an exciting and gratifying workplace."

STEVE GREENFIELD, INSTRUCTIONAL DEAN, MONTGOMERY COLLEGE, MARYLAND

■ ■ ■ ■ ■ ■ ■ ■ ■ ■

The Cornerstones of Engaging Leadership

Casey Wilson

MANAGEMENTCONCEPTS

ſſſ
MANAGEMENTCONCEPTS
8230 Leesburg Pike, Suite 800
Vienna, VA 22182
(703) 790-9595
Fax: (703) 790-1371
www.managementconcepts.com

Printed in the United States of America

Library of Congress Cataloging-in-Publication Data

Wilson, Casey.
    The cornerstones of engaging leadership / Casey Wilson.
       p. cm. -- (The Practical leader)
    ISBN 978-1-56726-218-6
1. Leadership. 2. Management. I. Title.
HD57.7.W537 2008
658.4'092--dc22

                                                        2007031152

10   9   8   7   6   5   4   3   2   1

About the Author

Casey Wilson is the Leadership and Management Practice Leader for Management Concepts. Management Concepts partners with individuals, groups, and organizations to improve performance through training, consulting, and publishing. In his role as Practice Leader, Mr. Wilson leverages his leadership expertise and background in consulting, adult learning, and instructional design to help others enhance their leadership capabilities.

Mr. Wilson also serves as an adjunct faculty member in the Human Resources and Management certificate program at Montgomery College, just outside of Washington, D.C., in Maryland. Mr. Wilson teaches courses on topics such as building high-performance work teams, successful interviewing skills for hiring and coaching, employee performance and conduct, and performance management.

Mr. Wilson earned a Master of Science in Leadership in Adult Education from the University of Wisconsin, Milwaukee, and a Bach-

elor of Science in Education from the University of Wisconsin,
Whitewater. He is a member of the American Society for Training
and Development (ASTD). He and his wife, Celene, live outside of
Washington, D.C.

To Celene, TJ, Abby, and our family, my cornerstones.

Table of Contents

Preface

Engagement—that was the word I had been trying to put my finger on for some time. It was powerful and suggestive in a way that attracts people to it with curiosity. Engagement is having passion, connectedness, motivation, and a willingness to give your best in order to benefit yourself and your organization. I read more on the topic of engagement, including the extensive research conducted by the Gallup Organization and the Corporate Leadership Council on organizational engagement and the implications of disengaged workforces. Each of these organizations uses a different framework to look at engagement, but both studies are very research and data-focused on an organizational level. Their research created the initial lens through which I viewed engagement.

Despite these studies, the general lack of data, models, and books on engaging leadership left me yearning for a practical, hands-on approach to becoming an engaging leader—the type of leader who actively and intentionally creates an engaging environment by connecting people to their work in meaningful ways. The research I'd come across so far did not provide a roadmap to actually becoming an engaging leader. I wanted to articulate, in a pragmatic way, *how* a person can become an engaging leader.

After exploring countless personal stories—from students in my classes, other consultants and facilitators, and leaders—I identified a few prominent, common threads related to engagement. These threads became the approach to engaging leadership I used as the foundation of this book. The approaches I present stem from real-life examples and personal experiences over time. I believe that they will resonate with people and cut-through some of the idealistic views that leadership books often take.

I've worked to provide an approach to engaging leadership that leaders at any organizational level can relate to—one that is practical and gets to the heart of what it means to be an engaging leader. Cutting through the trendy leadership jargon and selling points, I set out to write a book that would truly help all leaders, regardless of their title, experience, or number of colleagues.

Because engagement creates connections with and for others, this book focuses on what leaders can do both to monitor their own level of engagement and to engage others. To get the most out of this book, and to become an engaging leader, it's necessary to engage both your mind (through analytical, critical, and creative thinking) and your heart (through empathy and emotions).

Key elements of this book include:

- *The Engaging Leader Approach*—the model that serves as the foundation for this book, built by the four cornerstones of engaging leadership: building trust, understanding unique motivations, managing performance from a people-centric perspective, and engaging others' emotions.

- *Principles*—short, highlighted statements throughout the text that concisely convey key messages about engaging leadership.

- *Exercises*—opportunities to explore, reflect on, and practice key concepts and techniques, including self-assessments and self-reflective questions. The exercises can be used to clarify aspects of the engaging leader approach that are "internal" to you and focus on you as a leader. All the exercises are included on the supplemental CD that accompanies this book.

- *Practice Tools*—tools and techniques available to help you practice and apply the engaging leader approach. The focus of the practice tools is on external relationships and creating connections with others. Personalize or adapt them to meet individual needs as necessary. Practice tools are also included on the CD.

- *Stories*—real-world examples that convey the engaging leader approaches in action.

- *CD*—the tools, techniques, and exercises presented in the book, as well as additional resources, to print and use to become an engaging leader.

In my approach to engaging leadership, I have focused almost entirely on the interpersonal relationships leaders develop with others as a means for increasing engagement. I am looking forward to doing more work on how individuals' self-perceptions shape their engagement and how engaging leadership fits into larger organizational systems. I've touched on these topics briefly but recognize the need to offer more. Look for another book on each of these topics in the future.

While this book can help you become a more engaging leader, it is not a quick fix. It may change the way you see or think about things by providing insights, new frameworks, or even paths to success. However, bringing about visible, behavioral changes will require individual thought and action. Focus on making changes in areas within your control: It's not always possible to change organizational culture overnight, or to adjust processes and systems that are already firmly in place. But you *can* change what you as a leader hold yourself accountable for, especially the way you interact with others.

My own experience has brought the powerful feeling of being engaged. I also know the disappointment associated with not being engaged. You have probably had similar experiences. Time and time again I see "disconnects" between leaders and the people who work for them. These disconnects consistently foster disengagement. In my training and consulting work, I hear stories about leaders who completely ignore individuals' true needs, fostering cynicism and discontent. To get the best from people, leaders need to pay attention to individuals in a more holistic way. This way of leading benefits everyone.

Being an engaging leader can have a tremendous impact on you and on others, and I hope you decide to take steps toward becoming a leader who strives to build meaningful connections between individuals and their work. This book provides a pathway; the first step is yours to take.

Casey Wilson
Washington, D.C.

Acknowledgments

There are a lot of people who deserve my gratitude for supporting me while I wrote this book. I would like to acknowledge them and the organizations who helped with this project in one way or another—some intentionally and some not.

In October 2005 I attended a workshop called *Group Process Consultation* put on by the National Training Laboratories (NTL) Institute and facilitated by a man named Chuck Phillips. This experience was a turning point for me in the way I interacted with and engaged others. It gave me the practice and courage to truly listen to what people were saying and to figure out how to create connections with others. Chuck's wisdom, encouragement, and fostering of ownership for process-focused interventions and conversations was extremely influential.

In August 2006 I attended a workshop called *The* SPEED *of Trust* put on by CoveyLink, the consulting firm of Stephen M.R. Covey. I had met Stephen briefly at the American Society for Training and Development International Conference and was fascinated by his work on trust. The workshop, based on his book *The* SPEED *of Trust,* really opened my eyes to the many facets of trust. It is the one thing that leaders need if they want to get the best from others. I also want to thank Stephen for his testimonial for this book, which personally means a lot to me.

The Publishing team at Management Concepts—particularly Courtney Chiaparas, Myra Strauss, and Mary Cowell—have been a joy to work with. Their feedback, insights, and attention to detail along the way have helped *us* move this book along. Speaking of feedback, a number of people inside and outside the Management Concepts team read early drafts of the manuscript and offered their feedback. To each of you, thank you for your time, energy, and commitment to helping readers become engaging leaders.

Finally, I want to acknowledge my family and my wife, Celene, for their support. Writing a book isn't a one-person job. It takes nights and weekends and involves, at times, a bit of stress. Thank you for your patience, love, support, and engagement in the process.

A Perspective on Engagement

Dear Leader,

For the last few months I've been sitting at my desk feeling sapped of energy and passion for my work. I know, this isn't what you want to hear. After all, when I began my career here things were so promising. Do you remember?

Two years ago I was referred to our organization and was energized about the chance to work here. I knew that once I was hired, my talent and passion for what I do would shine through. I was finally going to be somewhere I could make a difference! This was my big opportunity.

After the first few months of sporadic training and random assignments, my excitement started to wane. My manager was a self-described "old-school manager." He'd been with the company for over 20 years. I learned early on that he was really in charge. In my third week he told me that all decisions were to go through him. He preferred to filter every communication, whether it be to a senior manager or a customer. Nobody on the team said anything to him about the way he made them feel, but I could tell my team-

mates were just going through the motions. I thought, "That won't be me. I am excited and ready to make a difference, no matter what!"

Fast forward ten months later to today. I am not happy with my job. My manager doesn't even really know me. He tries to motivate me by threatening me. Last week he said, "You'd better get that done. If you mess it up, there'll be hell to pay." I knew the hell he was referring to. Sally once missed a deadline and he yelled at her. I could hear him through his office walls! The sad thing is that it wasn't even Sally's fault. He'd told her the wrong deadline, and she was doing what he said. Now she doesn't trust him or anything he says.

All my frustration at work is starting to take a toll on my personal life, too. I am irritated when I get home from work. My friends know I am not excited about my job anymore and they console me by sending me postings for new positions. The thing is, I really wanted to work here. I really wanted to make a difference with—and for—this organization. But if nobody takes the time to connect with me—to care about me—then I just don't think I can do it. I am disengaging more and more every day. Leader, can you motivate me to use my talents and help the organization reach its goals? Would you, please?

Sincerely,
Becoming Disengaged

INTRODUCTION
Why Engaging Leadership? Why Now?

Thomas Edison once said, "If we all did the things we were capable of, we would literally astound ourselves." Actually, if leaders were able to engage others by tapping into their capabilities, talents, and potential, people would astound their leaders. Organizations are full of untapped potential; imagine what a thoroughly engaged, passionate, excited, willing, and happy workforce could accomplish. These are the characteristics of engaged people. The most engaging leaders create meaningful, positive connections with people to enable them to reach their potential and offer their best work.

To achieve the best performance and meet the changing demands and priorities of the 21st century workforce, leaders must be willing to unlearn the lessons of traditional leadership and find ways to differentiate their organizations—not through control or over-zealous processes, but through the talents of engaged individuals. The traditional command-oriented style of leadership has become obsolete. The world is changing at an unprecedented pace. The economic world market has increased our interdependency on change and global relationships. By the time organizations create and test perfect processes and policies, document them in an employee manual, and train individuals to use them consistently, the world has changed again and those processes and policies are no longer appropriate.

The changing landscape of 21st century organizations includes quickly changing business needs, greater numbers of retiring baby-boomers (creating a need for new, talented individuals to fill those roles), more employment opportunities in a competitive market, and new working conditions that promote telecommuting and work-life satisfaction. In addition to an increasingly competitive global market, the cultural interpretation of work has shifted. In the 21st century, a job is not just a job: it is a descriptor of personal identity, values, and beliefs. People want more from their jobs and they are willing to give greater efforts in exchange for more meaningful work. People will work harder if they are rewarded with the ability to contribute and influence.

The need to find meaning and to influence leads to a sense of engagement in work. People have higher expectations about the work they do, the meaning it creates for them, their sense of connection to it, and the harmony it creates in their lives.

■ ■ ■ ■ ■ ■ ■ ■ ■

"You don't lead people by hitting them over the head—that's assault, not leadership."

— DWIGHT D. EISENHOWER, U.S. PRESIDENT AND GENERAL

While many leaders may tout their employees as their greatest re-source, this is little more than lip service in many organizations. Many leaders are told to utilize the talents of others, but few are held accountable. Instead, the kind of personalized, individual attention that is necessary gives way to task-focused priorities. It is no surprise that this creates a cynical, disengaged workforce. When individuals become a mere part of a business landscape focused on results, it often means they are being neglected. As a result, increased numbers of individuals just float through their jobs on a day-to-day, week-to-week, and month-to-month basis, not feeling connected to their work or committed to their leaders.

As part of the evolving landscape of leadership in the 21st century, it is important to realize that the traditional command-oriented style of leadership is not engaging today's workforce. While in some organizations this style brings greater efficiency and consistency, it also marginalizes and shapes the contributions that individuals are willing to make. People do not perceive this style of leadership as mutually beneficial. Instead of inciting passion, innovation, creativity, and excitement, this approach has leaders trying to mold and shape everyone to be the same, which results in a group of employees acting more like inefficient machines than passionate, involved individuals.

Unlike times in history when jobs were scarce and options lacking, workers in the 21st century are inundated with numerous opportunities to find meaningful employment that meets their personal interests, needs, and priorities. Engagement fulfills the need for personal connections, including a sense of belonging, recognition, support, growth, and trust.

Traditional, command-oriented leadership will not provide organizations their best chance at success in the 21st century. Procedures and processes alone won't help them cope with the ever-changing world—people will. People are the difference and the competitive advantage. It is no wonder that a leadership approach that marginalizes individuals leads them to mentally check out of jobs. It is no wonder that individuals are not performing to their potential and using all their talents—their leaders are not engaging them. The new challenge for leaders at all organizational levels is to engage others to get their best efforts at work. In traditional thinking, command-oriented leadership works best. However, in the 21st century, people do not want to be controlled. They want to be engaged.

■ ■ ■ The Value of Engaged Individuals

What is the difference between passionate and dispassionate individuals within an organization? What is the difference between active engagement and active disengagement? Leaders at all levels of an organization should value engagement, as engagement has implications for every organizational level, including individual and group levels, and for the entire organization itself.

■ ■ ■ ■ ■ ■ ■ ■ ■

"Permanence is the last refuge of those with shriveled imaginations."

— WARREN BUFFETT, INVENTOR AND BUSINESSPERSON

■ ■ ■ ■ ■ ■ ■ ■ ■ ■

Actively engaged individuals enjoy greater job satisfaction and enrichment. They are excited to be at work and believe in the mission and vision of the organization. They find energy during stressful times, and they demonstrate a strong work ethic no matter how busy or slow the pace. Actively engaged individuals look at challenges differently and handle change more effectively. They are willing to resolve conflict and do so in a more productive way. They consistently focus on the quality of their work, no matter what the assignment. And they are committed to their work, their supervisors, and their organization.

Leaders have a vested interest in creating actively engaged teams as well. Not only do team members enjoy the same benefits collectively as they do on an individual level, but they also understand and appreciate the importance of increased collaboration, commitment, and trust. The more actively engaged a team is, the better it performs. In many organizations, teams and work groups drive important strategic and operational initiatives and projects, and these initiatives are influenced by the individual engagement of team or group members.

On an organizational level, actively engaged individuals provide a source of competitive advantage. They save resources through higher commitments to quality, less turnover, and increased productivity. They can also engage their customers through better service and higher quality standards, potentially leading to higher revenue.

▪ ▪ ▪ The Cost of Disengaged Individuals

To understand the implications of disengagement, consider the following research by some of the most respected research organizations in the world:

- The Gallup Organization estimates that disengagement costs $350 billion per year in lost productivity. In addition, its research suggests that health care costs increase when individuals are either non-engaged or actively disengaged, primarily due to stress, doctor visits, and physical problems—$350 billion![1]

- The Corporate Leadership Council, surveying 50,000 employees from 59 countries around the world, found that highly engaged individuals perform 20 percent better than non-engaged or actively disengaged individuals and are 87 percent less likely to leave their organizations. Furthermore, the council's analysis of rational and emotional forms of engagement indicates that emotional engagement drives individual discretionary effort four times greater than rational engagement.[2] Those are powerful numbers!

▪ ▪ ▪ ▪ ▪ ▪ ▪ ▪ ▪ ▪

"In motivating people, you've got to engage their minds and their hearts. It is good business to have a person feel part of the entire effort . . . I motivate people, I hope, by example—and perhaps by excitement, by having provocative ideas to make others feel involved."

— RUPERT MURDOCH, GLOBAL MEDIA EXECUTIVE AND BUSINESSPERSON

■ A study by Michael Treacy, author of *Double-Digit Growth: How Great Companies Achieve It No Matter What*, and his partners at Hewitt Associates indicates that companies with a 60 to 70 percent engaged workforce showed double the shareholder return of those with only a 49 to 60 percent engaged workforce. Companies with less than 25 percent of engaged people showed a negative shareholder return. This data shows that engagement not only affects individuals and leaders, it also affects customers and shareholders.[3]

As an engaging leader, it is imperative to understand the cost of disengagement, as the implications are tremendous. Actively disengaged individuals are more likely to leave an organization, resulting in higher levels of turnover. They use more sick time (which contributes to rising health care costs), decrease productivity, hurt team morale, and often frustrate customers. While engaged individuals focus on assignments and success, actively disengaged individuals focus on everything but the work. Their frustrations often bleed into their personal lives, too.

The data on disengagement is alarming when one considers what could be accomplished if an organization were to minimize active disengagement and transform non-engaged individuals into engaged employees. Temporarily, a leader may get by with only 25 percent member engagement driving group success; but what could be accomplished if more team members were engaged? Leaders cannot afford to depend on only those individuals who are currently engaged to produce the results necessary for business success. For maximum success, leaders must increase the number of engaged individuals working with them.

■ ■ ■ ■ ■ ■ **PRINCIPLE**

In the 21st century's global market, leaders cannot depend on only currently engaged individuals to produce successful results. It is necessary to increase engagement from others, too.

Whether recognizing the benefits of engagement from the perspective of individual potential or from a bottom-line perspective, leaders at all levels have a strong business case to care about—and work on—how they intentionally engage others, how they tap into the potential of others.

The groups with the most potential to become (or stay) engaged are the actively engaged and the non-engaged groups. This book presents methods for maintaining active engagement and inspiring non-engaged individuals to become engaged. It focuses less on what is necessary to transform actively disengaged individuals, because doing so typically drains a significant amount of energy with limited potential returns. Even managing to get actively disengaged individuals into the non-engaged category requires leaders to exert a tremendous amount of energy, and often at the cost of neglecting others.

■ ■ ■ What Can Engaging Leadership Accomplish?

What can engaging leadership accomplish when it positively shifts the percentage of non-engaged individuals, even if only a little? What if leaders could decrease the percentage of non-engaged individuals from 50 percent to 25 percent? By decreasing the number of non-engaged people by 25 percent and helping them join the existing 25 percent of engaged people, you could have over 50 percent of those working with you engaged. That would translate into a workforce where over half the people are engaged—over half the people working with the leader would be running on all cylinders, finding meaning and value in their work, and adding value to the organization. What could a leader—what could you—accomplish with that type of effort and commitment from people?

■ ■ ■ ■ ■ **EXERCISE**
Dreaming Big to Unleash the Potential of Others

This exercise is meant to give you a chance to dream big. Dreaming big means thinking of the bigger-picture goals or tasks you would like to accomplish. Think of the three biggest accomplishments you would like your work group to accomplish this year. Write them here:

1.

2.

3.

Now, ask yourself, "If I were able to tap into each group member's discretionary effort—if I were to get them all truly engaged—could I accomplish these goals?" Dream even bigger. Beyond the current goals listed above, what more could you accomplish by getting the best from others? Even more importantly, how would people feel if they were to accomplish those goals? Use this space to make a few notes:

Engagement is an individual choice people make, but engaging leaders are in the best position to influence the engagement levels of others. Engaging leaders resolve to not let others be disengaged or even non-engaged. Traditional thinking would suggest that leaders tell people to become engaged. But that traditional command-and-control approach actually fosters disengagement. Instead, engaging leaders find ways to create personal connections with others, connecting individuals to their work, to their organization, and to themselves as leaders by establishing high-quality relationships. Engaging leaders connect individuals in meaningful ways, tapping into their wants and needs, fostering a desire to take action.

■ ■ ■ ■ ■ ■ **PRINCIPLE**

Engaging leaders resolve to not let individuals disengage, but instead, proactively work to engage others.

ENDNOTES

1. The Gallup Organization, *The Gallup Management Journal*, http:// gmj.gallup.com/default.aspx (accessed August 15, 2007).
2. The Corporate Leadership Council, *Engaging the Workforce: Focusing on Critical Leverage Points to Drive Employee Engagement* (Washington, D.C.: The Corporate Executive Board, 2004).
3. Michael Treacy, *Double-Digit Growth: How Great Companies Achieve It No Matter What* (New York: The Penguin Group, 2003).

1 Engaging Leadership

It is imperative that leaders understand what engagement is, what engaging leadership is, how it can be used to foster engagement, and why engagement is critical to leaders and organizations. Engagement can be defined as a state of passion, connection, and motivation, and a willingness to give your best efforts to benefit yourself and your organization. Engaging leaders build trusting relationships, leverage unique motivations, take a people-centric approach to managing performance, and emotionally engage others. Engaging leadership gets the best results when it inspires others to use their discretionary effort in a way that is meaningful, positive, and results-oriented for the individual, the leader, and the organization.

You may be thinking, "This engagement stuff is only for executives or high-level leaders." After all, the far majority of literature on engagement focuses on data obtained at the organizational level. This data is mostly concerned with turnover and retention. While it is true that every executive- and high-level leader should pay attention to the engagement levels within their organization, leaders at every organizational level can influence engagement. This includes formal supervisors as well as those who take the lead in project teams, work groups, and in other co-worker interactions. Regardless of role or rank, all professionals have the ability to positively influence their interactions with others.

▪ ▪ ▪ Understanding and Exploring Engagement

Engagement is a state of being passionate, connected, motivated, and willing to give your best efforts to benefit yourself, your leader, and your organization. Every individual is engaged in some way, although their level of engagement may vary. The three different levels of engagement can be viewed on a continuum (see Figure 1-1). On one end of the continuum individuals are engaged, while on the opposite end of the continuum, individuals are actively disengaged.

▪ ▪ The Engaged Individual

Engaged individuals leverage their strengths to help themselves become high achievers. They proactively build relationships with oth-

---

FIGURE 1-1   Engagement Continuum

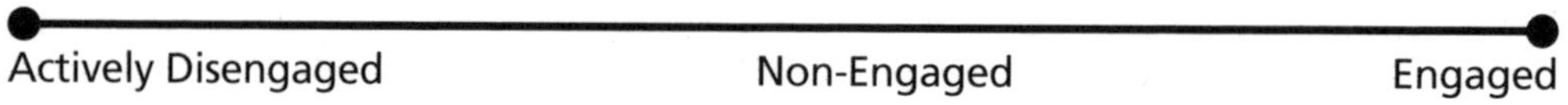

Actively Disengaged   Non-Engaged   Engaged

ers. They demonstrate commitment to their own development and success, the success of others, and the success of their organization. Engaged individuals have high aspirations, and they work positively and proactively to better understand their assignments and excel in them. When assignments are not available, they create work for themselves by volunteering for additional tasks. Energetic and enthusiastic, engaged individuals always seek to improve their effectiveness. They foster and facilitate conditions that contribute to their own success and to the success of others. An engaging environment is a catalyst for individual, group, and organizational success. Employee engagement can even drive customer engagement, stemming from highly positive and enjoyable experiences with engaged individuals.

Consider a time when you felt really tuned into your work, a time when you had a great relationship with a supervisor that was built on mutual trust. Your supervisor gave you challenging assignments and rewarded you in ways that made you feel valuable. In essence, the supervisor knew how to inspire your best effort and performance. By working together, you fed off of each other's excitement and energy. In other words, you were engaged in your work.

■ ■ The Non-Engaged Individual

Non-engaged individuals are neither actively engaged nor actively disengaged; they are neutral. Non-engaged individuals do not invest much effort in going the extra mile for themselves, nor for internal or external customers. They tend not to be innovative. And while they do not necessarily work against their organization, they do not proactively work to better it either. Many just hang out, biding their time day-in and day-out, simply riding the work wave.

Non-engaged individuals make up the majority of the modern work-force. Because this group is simply floating along, they are the group with the most potential to become engaged. Leaders should spend the most effort trying to engage this group of people. This potential exists because these individuals are not frustrated and jaded, as are actively disengaged employees. Instead, they haven't had a leader who sparked their sense of passion and excitement.

Visualize a teeter totter—one of those dizzying playground rides where kids ride up and down until they practically fall off. If engaged individuals are the ones who are "up," and actively disengaged individuals are "down," non-engaged individuals are right in the middle. Their ups and downs are not quite as dramatic. However, because of their neutral position on the teeter totter, they can potentially slide to either side—up or down. Leaders have the potential to engage this group in the middle so that they join side that's "up."

The Actively Disengaged Individual

Actively disengaged individuals thrive on negativity. They give the minimum amount of effort possible because they perceive that nobody cares about them or what they do at work. They arrive each day, perform a little work—typically work of lower quality compared to engaged individuals—and leave. They display negativity by complaining and nagging. They are purposely contrary, often going against the grain. When given feedback, they ignore it. Actively disengaged individuals let everyone know about their unhappiness, and some even try to perpetuate negativity in hopes of getting others to join them—sort of a "misery loves company" perspective.

Active disengagement occurs when individuals feel they work under negative or toxic work conditions, perceive their supervisors to be insensitive, and have unmet emotional needs. They feel subjected to office politics that distract them from their goals, or they feel they are not receiving individual attention in a meaningful way. This lack of personalized attention can cause resentment and be a catalyst for "checking out" of work.

Current data suggests that most individuals working in organizations are not actively engaged (see Figure 1-2).[1] The percentages in this figure were determined by an informal meta-analysis of three different studies on engagement by three different organizations.

FIGURE 1-2   Employee Engagement Percentages in Organizations

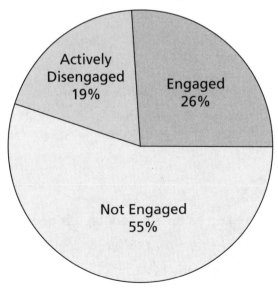

Looking at the percentages of people within a given workforce, there are a number of interesting points:

- Only about one-fourth of people are passionate, committed, and connected to their work.
- What is worse, about one-fifth of people are working against their organizations through active disengagement!
- Setting aside those two ends of the continuum, over half of people are simply floating through their work days, not working against their organizations but also not feeling connected and committed.
- Knowing that engaged people give their best work to their organizations, about three-fourths of people have some amount of discretionary effort they are not giving to their organization or their leader.

Discretionary effort is the amount of energy kept in reserves that someone chooses to use or not depending on how they feel about their work. Every person has a certain amount of discretionary effort. High performers bring plenty of discretionary effort to the table, and most leaders wish all their colleagues brought just as much.

Everyone has a certain amount of discretionary effort they can choose to deliberately leverage—or not leverage—on behalf of their leader.

■ ■ ■ ■ ■ ■ PRINCIPLE

Engaging leaders believe in people. It is people and their use of discretionary effort that differentiate high-performing organizations from the rest.

Leaders who successfully engage people can tap into their discretionary effort. Without draining that reservoir of discretionary effort, engaging leaders find ways to replenish it. Think of engagement and discretionary effort as renewable resources. With an engaging leader, people are inspired to achieve more. For many organizations, the quality, commitment, and passion of their employees drives the effort to accomplish all missions.

Engaging leaders must believe in people. Today, individual talent and a willingness to exert discretionary efforts differentiate successful organizations from the rest.

■ ■ ■ ■ ■ **EXERCISE**
When Have You Been Engaged? (Using a Career Line)

In order for leaders to engage others, they must be engaged themselves. This is important because individuals who have engaged supervisors are more likely to be engaged themselves, and they are also more likely to understand what it takes to be engaged. That said, non-engaged supervisors will find it difficult to engage others.

This exercise can help you better understand your own levels of engagement throughout your career. The objective is for you to consider periods of your career when you were engaged or disengaged, and why.

First select a period of time to analyze (e.g., the past five years of a current position). The straight printed line represents the time when you were not engaged. Now draw peaks and valleys relative to the printed line: peaks for times when you were highly engaged, parallel lines for times when you were not engaged but not actively disengaged, and valleys for times when you were actively disengaged. Label those peaks and valleys. Take a few minutes to note why you were engaged at those peak times. Make notes similarly for times when you were non-engaged or actively disengaged.

Example:

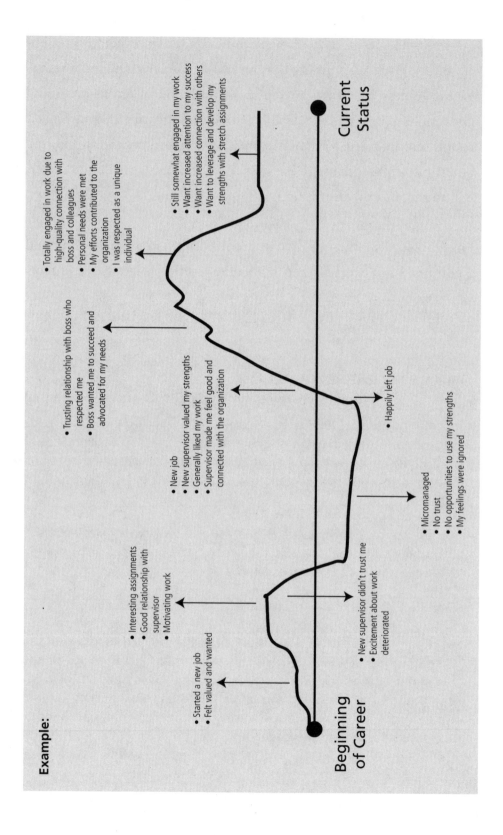

Beginning of Career

- Started a new job
- Felt valued and wanted

- Interesting assignments
- Good relationship with supervisor
- Motivating work

- New supervisor didn't trust me
- Excitement about work deteriorated

- Micromanaged
- No trust
- No opportunities to use my strengths
- My feelings were ignored

- Happily left job

- New job
- New supervisor valued my strengths
- Generally liked my work
- Supervisor made me feel good and connected with the organization

- Trusting relationship with boss who respected me
- Boss wanted me to succeed and advocated for my needs

- Totally engaged in work due to high-quality connection with boss and colleagues
- Personal needs were met
- My efforts contributed to the organization
- I was respected as a unique individual

- Still somewhat engaged in my work
- Want increased attention to my success
- Want increased connection with others
- Want to leverage and develop my strengths with stretch assignments

Current Status

Your Career Line:

_____

Beginning   **Today**

Analyzing Your Career Line

Look at the peaks on your career line. What made those moments high
points in your career? What was it about the organization, and more
specifically, about your leader, that helped you reach those points? How did
your leader help you? What was the relationship like?

Now consider the valleys on your career line. Why were they low points?
What did the organization or leader do to contribute to those low points?
What do you wish they would have done differently?

Similar to the stock market, individual engagement levels may go up and
down depending on the amount of energy and time invested in the person.
Consider the leaders who have taken the time to invest in you. How do
those experiences relate to your job satisfaction at the time? What about
the leaders who only took your hard work without investing anything back
into you? It's very likely that those experiences relate to the low points on
your career line and were times when you wanted to be engaged, but were
not. Engaging leaders create meaningful connections and invest in the
successes of others.

▪ ▪ ▪ How to Increase Engagement

Individuals can become engaged in two ways: through self-directed engagement and through engaging leadership. For most, sustaining self-directed engagement requires the personal connections that come from an engaging leader. Individuals ultimately choose how to use their discretionary effort, but leaders should seek out and facilitate mutually beneficial ways to inspire them to use such effort. Engaging leadership is about tapping into an individual's potential to allow greater and more satisfying results for themselves, their leaders, and their organizations.

Through intentional actions and specific behaviors, leaders can increase engagement and tap into the discretionary energy of others. It is important to for leaders to recognize that both their abilities and their rapport with others directly influence success levels. The stronger the interpersonal connection, the better the chance a person will be willing to engage.

▪ ▪ ▪ ▪ ▪ ▪ PRINCIPLE

A strong interpersonal connection with a leader is the primer for individual engagement.

Developing strong interpersonal connections requires leaders to have a biopic perspective. Through one lens leaders are mindful of their intentions, actions, and behaviors; through the second lens, they create personal connections and relationships with others.

The First Lens: Self-Mindfulness

The engaging leader approach is built on mindfulness of self and of others. Being mindful is being aware of internal thoughts, feelings, emotions, and reactions. It is also being aware of the thoughts, feelings, emotions, and reactions of others. Being mindful means listening to an inner voice and willingly and intentionally finding ways to connect with others on a meaningful, personal level.

Self-mindfulness is important to engagement for a number of reasons. First and foremost, leaders are the primary role model for others—and people do monitor their leaders' engagement levels. While this monitoring may not be explicit or intentional, people nevertheless pick up on their leaders' engagement vibes. They notice levels of trust in the organization, methods of managing performance, and levels of emotional engagement. The more leaders engage, the more likely they will be to inspire others to engage. Therefore, it is critical for leaders to monitor their own level of engagement to make sure it models well for others.

The second reason mindfulness is important is because in order to truly engage others, a leader must get to know and understand them. Self-exploration gives a leader practice at finding an inner voice and deeper thoughts and emotions. It requires leaders to ask themselves some challenging questions about the implications of trust or distrust in their own work relationships; about their preferences when others manage their performance; and about the extent to which they are emotionally connected to their work. Once leaders know themselves well, they are more likely to empathize with others as they explore and articulate their own needs. Asking themselves challenging questions will make it easier to ask others the same kinds of questions.

While it is not easy, leaders can become more mindful through self-awareness, self-understanding, and self-management. *Self-awareness* occurs as leaders become aware of personal opinions, thoughts, feelings, preferences, and heuristics. Heuristics are unconscious routines that individuals develop in their lives. They are hard-wired into the brain, and because of this, people often fail to recognize them. Instead, they often believe that everyone shares their world view and sees things the same way as themselves. Just recognizing that these tendencies exist is the first step toward understanding them and their influence on individual thoughts and actions.

Self-understanding occurs when leaders take their self-awareness and known heuristics and explore them to better comprehend how they shape personal perspectives, character, and leadership approaches. Understanding their own leadership approach allows leaders to actively and consciously make choices about how to interact with others. It can also facilitate a better understanding of how others perceive their leader. This kind of self-understanding is necessary for leaders to achieve congruence between who they are and who they want to be.

The congruence that an individual seeks as a leader happens through action, which is where *self-management* takes place. If awareness is the internal recognition of yourself and understanding is the internal comprehension of it, then self-management is the part most visible to others. This is because people more easily recognize actions and behaviors (as opposed to thoughts). For example, if a leader is consistently playing to peoples' strengths, it will likely be noticed. These visible behaviors allow leaders to build more effective and engaging relationships.

Getting to know yourself can be a scary process, but it does not have to be. Think of it as an iterative process over time. Individuals live and learn, which requires their perspectives, preferences, opinions, and approaches to evolve with time.

Engaging leaders can take advantage of many ways to develop self-awareness and self-understanding, each of which is a step toward more effective self-management. Self-assessments are a great place to start. Effective self-assessments provide a framework for learning about yourself, and yourself in relation to others. Some particularly helpful self-assessments include:

- Myers-Briggs Type Indicator® (MBTI®)
- Fundamental Interpersonal Relations Orientation-Behavior™ (FIRO-B®)
- SPEED of Trust® Audit
- Emotional Intelligence Self Appraisal™

In addition to self-assessments (which risk incorporating significant amount of personal bias when individuals lack self-awareness or are not honest about personal shortcomings), multi-rater assessments, such as a 360-degree feedback assessment, are quite valuable. Multi-rater assessments allow participants to recognize personal traits they may not have been aware of previously. Being aware of these blind spots and understanding them can lead to increased congruence between personal thoughts and corresponding actions or behaviors. It may also highlight the need for self-work. The self-awareness that comes as a result of these assessments often requires individual flexibility and a willingness to adjust previous leadership approaches.

Engaging leaders can become self-aware in other ways as well. For example, journaling can be helpful in capturing a state of mind, including thoughts on physical and emotional reactions to situations. However, journaling is only helpful if writers revisit and explore their entries and learn from them afterwards. Thinking about what happened and *why* can be insightful, and if done with an open mind, can lead to greater self-understanding and more effective choices.

Another way to become more self-aware is to have open discussions and forums on important topics. Numerous topics can generate thought-provoking discussions, including personal leadership philosophies, past practices from leaders who did or did not engage people, what people like and dislike most about their work as a leader, the role that trust plays in working with others, what unique motivators each person has, and how people prefer to be managed. These discussions can help participants discover other helpful points of view.

Forging personal connections with others also requires that leaders be genuine and be perceived as genuine. Only through honest, direct, and genuine conversations can leaders engage others.

■ ■ ■ ■ ■ ■ PRINCIPLE

> To be authentic and genuine, you must understand who you are (and who you are not) and who you want to be as a leader.

Former PepsiCo CEO Roger Enrico said, "Beware of the tyranny of small changes to small things. Rather, make big changes to big things." Becoming an engaging leader may mean making big changes, and it is a choice each leader has to make. Engaging leaders do not cheapen themselves by simply going through the motions; instead, they buy into the importance and value of self-mindfulness and authenticity when working with others. Being social is a part of that authenticity and a part of the human experience. Sometimes leaders lose sight of the need for human connection. Becoming engaging may require a willingness to reconnect with the human side of the workplace or in some cases to reinvent one's self with a renewed sense of conviction to be authentic and genuine.

■■■■■■■■■■

"One day, out of nowhere, you realize you don't know who you are, and none of the cards in your wallet provide the slightest clue to your real identity."

— SAM KEEN, *FIRE IN THE BELLY*

■■■■■■■■■■

■■ The Second Lens: Creating Personal Connections and Relationships

Through the second lens, leaders must view personal connections and relationships as the primary vehicle for engaging others. This may require a fundamental paradigm shift in the way leaders think about their colleagues: Rather than think about their colleagues only as knowledge workers, they must recognize them as human beings who have personal goals, desires, and needs. This makes creating connections and building relationships critical. If leaders want their colleagues to be loyal and committed, they must reciprocate that loyalty and commitment. The only way to achieve this is through meaningful, positive personal connections and strong relationships.

Leaders must take four key actions to connect with and engage others. These key actions are the four cornerstones of engaging leadership:

- Build trust as the foundation of effective relationships.
- Motivate individuals in ways that are uniquely meaningful to them.
- Take a people-centric approach to managing performance.
- Engage the emotions of others in their work.

Engaging leaders demonstrate self-mindfulness while creating personal connections with others. Each of the four cornerstones of engaging leadership involves self-mindfulness and creating personal connections.

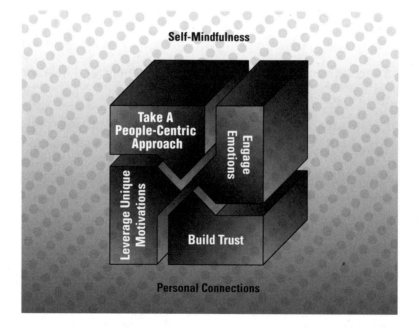

Each of the subsequent four sections of this book is dedicated to one of the cornerstones of engaging leadership. Leaders can become more effective by making any one of these a serious priority. But by separating the cornerstones, an important element is lost. Combining these principles through the lens of engagement will unleash the true potential of others and inspire effective performances and an amazing sense of pride and commitment, enabling individuals and organizations to achieve their best results.

By building trust, understanding unique motivations, managing performance from a people-centric perspective, and engaging emotions, engaging leaders can tap into the true potential of others. This humanistic approach creates situations where engaging leaders, their colleagues, and their organizations all benefit. By shifting a paradigm of what it means to lead others, engaging leaders can create connections and ensure success at all levels of an organization.

If leaders want to fully engage others, they must recognize each individual's unique needs and preferences. To use an analogy, engagement is like food and each of the four cornerstones of engaging leadership is a bite of nourishment. Individuals want and need different portions, and they are hungry for them at different times. Some prefer smaller bites of many different foods, while others prefer large bites of a single kind of food. Some individuals want the sampler platter, while others want to gulp down the entire meal! No preference here is necessarily right or wrong, only more or less satisfying for any given person.

> "Nobody can prevent you from choosing to be exceptional."
>
> — MARK SANBORN, *THE FRED FACTOR*

■ ■ ■ ■ ■ PRACTICE TOOL
Exploring the Engagement of Others

This tool offers a series of questions to help determine whether you are engaging others. Each of the questions correlates with a specific cornerstone of engaging leadership. You may already know in your heart whether or not you are engaging others, but if you do not know or if you want to confirm your suspicions, this questionnaire provides a good way to start thinking about it.

Think about your current team or the group of people you currently influence. List their names here:

Below each of the following questions is a continuum. For each question and its respective continuum, consider the question and write someone's name on the continuum in the appropriate place. Instead of thinking of your responses as right or wrong, think of them in terms of more or less.

Example:

Q. 1 Can you say with confidence that this person trusts you?

Ahmed   Omar   Joe   Jessica

●————————————————————————————————————●

No – Distrusts Me   **Yes – Trusts Me**

BUILDING TRUST

Q. 1 Can you say with confidence that this person trusts you?

●————————————————————————————————————●

No – Distrusts Me   **Yes – Trusts Me**

LEVERAGING UNIQUE MOTIVATORS

Q. 2 Can you describe the three most personal motivators for this person?

●──●

I Cannot   I Can

ENGAGING EMOTIONS

Q. 3 Do you feel comfortable expressing emotions with this person at work?

●──●

No – Uncomfortable   Yes – Comfortable

A PEOPLE-CENTRIC APPROACH TO MANAGING PERFORMANCE

Q. 4 How often do you give recognition to this person?

●──●

Quarterly   Weekly

LEVERAGING UNIQUE MOTIVATORS

Q. 5 How well do you know this person's interests outside of work?

●──●

Not Well   Extremely Well

A PEOPLE-CENTRIC APPROACH TO MANAGING PERFORMANCE

Q. 6 When was the last time you complimented this person for a specific strength they possess?

●──●

This Year   This Week

A PEOPLE-CENTRIC APPROACH TO MANAGING PERFORMANCE

Q. 7 How often do you ask this person for their opinion?

●──●

Not Often   Frequently

A PEOPLE-CENTRIC APPROACH TO MANAGING PERFORMANCE

Q. 8 How often do you intentionally give assignments that leverage this person's strengths?

Not Often   **Frequently**

LEVERAGING UNIQUE MOTIVATORS

Q. 9 When was the last time you explicitly discussed motivation with this person?

Never   **This Week**

A PEOPLE-CENTRIC APPROACH TO MANAGING PERFORMANCE

Q. 10 When was the last time your gave this person honest, direct feedback about his or her performance?

This Month   **This Week**

ENGAGING EMOTIONS

Q. 11 According to your perception, how interested is this person's in his or her work?

Not Very Interested   **Very Interested**

This exercise is not meant to highlight your particular skills or abilities as a leader; it simply provides a way to begin thinking about how you engage others. Your responses to these questions should provide some insight into your level of engaging leadership with the people you listed.

Each of the questions above correlates with a specific cornerstone of engaging leadership. If you find that you are not practicing one of the cornerstones, pay special attention to the particular chapter of the book to get practical tips and techniques for improvement. Then again, you may find that you are already engaging others fairly well. Depending on how your responses fell on the continuum, you may have additional opportunities to engage others.

ENDNOTE

1. Data was gathered from: *The Gallup Management Journal* (The Gallup Organization, The Gallup Management Journal, http://gmj.gallup.com/default.aspx.); The Corporate Leadership Council (The Corporate Leadership Council, *Engaging the Workforce: Focusing on Critical Leverage Points to Drive Employee Engagement* (Washington, D.C.: The Corporate Executive Board, 2004)); and Developmental Dimensions International (Paul Bernthal, Ph.D., Richard S. Wellins, Ph.D., and Mark Phelps, *Employee Engagement: The Key to Realizing Competitive Advantage* (Pittsburgh: Developmental Dimensions International, Inc., 2005).

RECOMMENDED READING

Boyatzis, Richard E., and Annie McKee. *Resonant Leadership: Renewing Yourself and Connecting with Others through Mindfulness, Hope, and Compassion*. Boston: Harvard Business School Press, 2005.

Carlson, Peg, Anne Davidson, Sue McKinney, and Roger Schwarz. *The Skilled Facilitator Field Book: Tips, Tools, and Tested Methods for Consultants, Facilitators, Managers, Trainers, and Coaches*. San Francisco: Jossey-Bass, 2005.

Senge, Peter. *The Fifth Discipline*. New York: Doubleday, 1990.

Senge, Peter. *The Fifth Discipline Field Book*. New York: Doubleday, 1994.

2 Building and Maintaining Trust

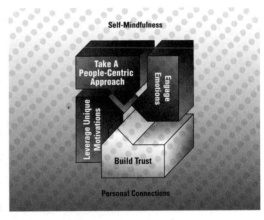

In engaging leadership, trust is the interpersonal care and intentional acknowledgment of individual values, motivations, and needs. Trust is the foundation of engaging leadership. Without trust, leaders cannot fully engage others because when individuals give their best and are fully engaged, they are also putting themselves at risk. They risk trying but failing, giving but not receiving in return, and caring deeply without reciprocation. Without a trusting relationship with their leader, individuals often think they have too much to risk to be actively and passionately engaged.

To be committed, passionate, and motivated, and to give the discretionary effort necessary to engage, individuals need to trust their leader to respect such efforts. Without trust, attempts to motivate, to take a people-centric approach to managing performance, or to emotionally engage others will all be futile. Distrusted leaders are consistently questioned and are the subject of much cynicism. Even when trying to act engaging, those who work with a leader they don't trust may wonder, "Why is my leader acting this way? What does he want? What is his motive?" Instead of feeling valued, individuals may feel used and suspicious. Simply put, engagement does not work without trust.

When trust is present in relationships, though, leaders and their colleagues thrive. They cooperate, share information and expertise, discuss issues openly, and work harder to meet expectations. These elements are the foundation of an engaging relationship.

■ ■ ■ ■ ■ ■ PRINCIPLE

Trust is the foundation of engaging leadership.

In the context of engagement, trust is based on the relationships leaders build with others. Engagement involves passion, connectedness, motivation, and a willingness to work hard to achieve maximum potential. Those who truly want to engage must trust those around them, particularly their leader. Trust affects individual relationships as well as group or even organizational relationships. In a world of constant change, trust is the glue that binds leaders to those around them.

"Trust is like the air we breathe.

When it's present, nobody really notices.

But when it's absent, everybody notices."

— WARREN BUFFETT, INVENTOR AND BUSINESSPERSON

Consider the following divergent examples of experiences related to taking on a new assignment. In the first situation, supervisor Josephina has shown a penchant for being self-interested. She constantly hides mistakes and downplays errors when it comes to her work. She loves to take high-profile assignments that make her look good. When an assignment with the potential to explode comes up, she delegates it to a staff member so that she can pass the buck if necessary. Everyone else on the team has experienced this. When she approaches someone about taking on a new assignment, their first question is, "What's wrong with the assignment that she doesn't want to do it?" No one *trusts* her to keep their best interests in mind.

In another situation, supervisor Jose has consistently demonstrated a genuine interest in making sure his colleagues are delegated high-quality assignments, asking for their opinion when delegating work, and recognizing tough assignments when they come up. As a team member walks into his office, Jose says, "I've got a great assignment for you, if you want it. Do you have a few minutes to talk about it?" The team member does not first react by wondering what is wrong with the assignment. Instead, he or she thinks, "I know Jose is looking out for me. I wonder what this assignment is; it sounds interesting." His teammates *trust* Jose to consider their best interests.

Notice the difference between these two situations. When individuals trust one another, they are willing to open up, take chances, and give more of their discretionary effort. Implicit in trying to engage others is the notion that others will reciprocate and open up in return; they will share their thoughts, their motivations, and their dreams, and they will trust their leaders to take these personal elements into consideration at all times. While leaders may not base actions or decisions on these personal elements every time, they at least *recognize* them. This recognition and acknowledgment increases trust.

▪▪▪ The Benefits of Trust

Trust works when individuals lose self-motivated, self-serving attitudes and focus on contributing to groups and achieving goals through collaboration. This is a huge step emotionally and intellectually, and it involves risk. That said, leaders must convince others it is a risk worth taking by explicitly highlighting the benefits of building trusting relationships.

Building trust reduces the time and effort needed to manage others while enhancing the quality of their work and self-perceived value. Trust breaks down the traditional walls between leaders and others. Trusting relationships increase cooperation, foster creativity, allow quality feedback, and contribute to dynamic and synergistic relationships.

▪▪ Measuring the Cost of Distrust

People often think of trust in black or white terms: either you trust someone or you do not. But trust in a relationship is rarely that simple; it almost always occurs in shades of gray. Individuals have different levels of trust. Someone may trust someone else with one thing, but not with another. Trust is often perceived as one of those elusive qualities that cannot be measured. Actually, trust and distrust *can* be measured, and leaders should take note of the cost of distrust.

Have you heard the old saying: "People don't leave organizations, they leave supervisors"? Why do people leave their supervisors? Usually because issues of trust have arisen on some level. For example, someone may not trust their supervisor to look out for their best interests if they never receive attractive assignments nor receive meaningful feedback. Therefore, they leave the leader in search of a more trusting, reciprocal relationship. Similarly, someone may not trust their supervisor to advocate for a well-deserved raise. Or they may not trust their supervisor to be forthright and honest. Each of these situations demonstrates what might compel a person to leave one job in search of another, to seek an environment where effective and honest communication—hallmarks of a trusting relationship—take place.

Regardless of its causes, distrust may cost the organization an employee. Considering that the average cost of recruiting and selecting a new employee is equivalent to about one year's salary, the cost of distrust can add up quickly if it means higher turnover rates.

Distrust has other costs. For example, unproductive meetings caused by a lack of trust can be a huge sinkhole of resources. Meetings that include a discussion about every single detail of a project because members do not trust their teammates to do their jobs correctly, for example, can be very expensive. Consider four people earning $25 per hour in an unnecessary meeting for one hour: the cost of that meeting is $100. Say there are four meetings spurred by distrust in a single week. That wastes $400 per week, or over $20,000 per year. And that is just one team; consider the impact such meetings have on an entire organization. The monetary cost of distrust can add up quickly.

Stephen M.R. Covey's *The SPEED of Trust*[1] looks at trust using the analogy of a trust tax and a trust dividend. Great trust pays dividends: Individuals work harder for each other and things happen much faster. Distrust taxes the individuals involved, and the tax can be a heavy one, sometimes reducing the potential dividend by half! This simple analogy highlights why trust is so important for making progress and how its absence can be such a heavy burden on leaders.

Trust fails individuals when their leaders, their team, or their organization does not live up to the standards, values, and ethical behavior they expect. Once individuals sense that their needs are not being considered, distrust starts to grow. Like a weed, it finds its way into the cracks of teams and organizations. Engaging leaders work to actively exterminate the weeds of distrust.

■ ■ ■ Factors that Influence Trust

A better understanding of trust and distrust comes from exploring the factors that influence our trust in others. These factors relate to engaging leadership because individual decisions to contribute discretionary effort are in part based on whether they consider their leaders trustworthy. Without awareness of and attention to these influencing factors, leaders can miss an opportunity to strengthen relationships and increase engagement.

■ ■ History and Experience

We often trust someone who consistently demonstrates certain behaviors. This consistency allows us to minimize our risks by predicting future behaviors. For example, if a leader consistently rejects the notion that leaders should act friendly and empathetic, a coworker can reasonably assume that these behaviors will continue. Therefore, instead of investing effort to convince the leader to be empathetic, the coworker assumes these behaviors will continue. If the leader does act friendly, the coworker may not trust the leader's motives or intentions in light of the inconsistent behaviors being demonstrated.

The movie *Apollo 13* famously portrays the true story of the lunar-landing mission, when three astronauts were stranded in a crippled space shuttle on their way to the moon. In the movie, one of the characters—James Lovell—utters those now-famous words, "Houston, we have a problem," alerting NASA headquarters to emergent mechanical difficulties. In their time of need, the crew turns to Ken Mattingly to save them. Their decision is not random: They trust him with their lives because of his experience and their history with him.

This example reiterates how personal history and experience with others play a role in trust. For years prior to this mission, Mattingly had trained to be an astronaut and a member of the Apollo 13 crew. About three days prior to launch, Mattingly was exposed to German measles and was removed from flight status. With problems on the shuttle, the crew turned to Mattingly and his experience to help them. The crew trusted him because of their history with him.

In the workplace, trust based on history and experience manifests itself in many ways. We look to consistent performers and colleagues whose behavior we can predict—which translates into a level of trustworthiness. However, when individuals act erratically, demonstrating changing behaviors, moods, or actions, it becomes difficult to predict how they will act, and thus our history and experience with them demonstrates that they are less trustworthy. This link between consistent behavior and trust also applies in determining whether or not to trust a leader.

■ ■ ■ ■ ■ **EXERCISE**
Considering the Influence of History on Trust

To bring to life the idea that history plays a factor in our trust in others, take a few minutes to think about the following examples. The goal of the exercise is for you to consider, from your own experiences, how your history with people played a factor in your trust in them.

For each situation, think of a specific time in the past when someone behaved in this way. Then think about how this action affected your level of trust in the person.

☐ Pulled through on a large assignment for you

☐ Let you down

☐ Took an action that you understood and felt comfortable with

☐ Took an action that you did not understand and feel comfortable with

☐ Broke your confidence

☐ Confided in you

☐ Withheld information from you

☐ Kept a promise to you

☐ Said one thing but did another

Since that time, how has your trust increased or decreased? Why?

Our past experiences with others shape the way we interact with them in the future. For an engaging leader, this has significant implications—the biggest being that there is no day like today to begin building more trusting relationships. Your future success depends on the trusting relationships you build today.

Competence and Ability

Our assessment of individual competence and ability with a given task is another factor that influences our level of trust. We have all known someone who strongly wants to do something but lacks the ability to do it properly. For example, your 14-years-old child may have an extremely strong desire to drive the family car; that does not mean you trust her ability to drive the car.

Similarly, simply because an individual is competent does not mean that person can be trusted. For example, if a colleague offers to drive your brand new car to the car wash for you, his competence as a car driver does not mean that you would automatically trust him to do so.

Our own experiences teach us that competence and ability are factors influencing trustworthiness. Leaders perceived as competent garner trust more easily than those who are perceived as incompetent. For example, consider a leader who serves in an accountant role. If he is unable to balance the books and is not up-to-date on financial laws, policies, and procedures, he will have a hard time convincing his team to trust him. If that leader is to engender the trust of the other professionals, particularly when assigning work, he needs to demonstrate a level of competence.

Competency and ability play a large role in an individual's willingness to trust a leader. Engaging leaders should consider themselves from the perspective of others and ask themselves whether others will trust their competency and ability.

Similarities and Differences

Individuals who share similarities with others find it easier to trust one another, mainly because individuals tend to trust themselves. Therefore, people usually associate similarities with trust. For example, a few colleagues following the same career paths at a company may naturally gravitate toward each other with trust because they can empathize and relate to shared or similar experiences.

Conversely, when individuals differ and do not understand another perspective or experience, their defenses often go up and their trust decreases. This is not to say that differing individuals are necessarily untrustworthy or that they cannot establish trust. In fact, it is possible to establish trusting relationships with others who may be difficult by demonstrating respect and intentionally creating shared understanding. Nevertheless, differences are often a perceived barrier to developing trust.

Power and Authority

Another factor affecting trust is personal power or authority. In the workplace, it may be difficult to develop a sense of trust with someone who controls things like promotional opportunities, compensation, or work assignments—unless the individual is considered benevolent. The implication for leaders is that some individuals have an us-versus-them view of relationships with ranking colleagues. The key factor influencing how others perceive personal power or authority is *how* it is used. Leaders can influence how others think about their power, influence, and authority through their actions.

For example, a leader who lets his or her title "go to his or her head" may act with little regard for others' opinions. An example is the leader who bullies others into accepting his or her approach to everything. While positional authority may allow the leader to require others to adopt his or her practices, it may generate unhealthy views of the leader. While a leader does not have to constantly bend toward others' preferences, he or she must be aware of how others view his or her approach to leadership and recognize the implications. This self-mindfulness of how power or authority is viewed can lead to more thoughtful actions and approaches that build trust rather than erode it.

Organizational Culture

When focusing on the facets of trust within a leader's sphere of control, it is important to note the effects of organizational culture. Social norms, imposed structures and processes, and discouraging climates often force themselves upon individuals, minimizing the opportunity to develop genuine trust. When organizations value processes over individuals, it is often interpreted as a lack of benevolence. When they do not follow through on their commitments, organizations can foster a culture of frustration, anxiety, and toxicity. Organizations that do not keep their word—whether by failing to accomplish a mission or by not following through on commitments—push their employees toward distrust and disengagement.

Benevolence

Of all the factors that influence trust in the engaging leader approach, benevolence is the most critical. Benevolence translates into personal concern for the welfare of others. Non-benevolent leaders have a much harder time gaining trust than their benevolent counterparts, because individuals simply do not trust someone who does not care about their best interests. Individual willingness to engage is often greatly diminished if personal efforts are not reciprocated; this often becomes a significant reason for disengagement, too. If you were to think about and describe three actively disengaged individuals, you would undoubtedly note that they all believe their leader is non-benevolent.

Questions someone might ask when considering whether a leader is benevolent include:

■ Does my leader share responsibility so that I can grow in my role?

■ Does my leader ask me about my family and how I am doing?

■ Does my leader share control of workplace decisions that affect me?

■ Does my leader recognize me for who I really am?

■ ■ ■ ■ ■ ■ **PRINCIPLE**

In the 21st century workforce, benevolence has the greatest influence on trust in relationships between leaders and others.

▪▪▪ Building Trust

It can be difficult to build trusting relationships. It is critical, though, to lay this foundation when working on engagement. A perceived intention to build trust plays a role in developing these relationships, but genuine care *plus* intention—that is, illustrating "good character"—is the glue that holds specific trust-building behaviors together. Genuine care and intention both need to be present because a leader may intentionally try to build trust with others, but if he or she does not truly care about others as people and as professionals, they will know. Or, vice versa, a person may care about an individual, but if he or she does not work to intentionally build a trusting relationship, the relationship may not be as strong as possible. An engaging leader will show genuine care and work to establish a trusting relationship.

Trust is the foundation of engagement. During any given week, leaders have hundreds of interactions with a variety of people. With each of these interactions, engaging leaders have an opportunity to build trust. While trust may seem to be a hard thing to define and truly grasp, there are some specific behaviors leaders can demonstrate to build trust. Figure 2-1 lists trust-building behaviors and cross-references them to the cornerstones of engaging leadership.

FIGURE 2-1 Trust-Building Behaviors

Trust-Building Behavior	Examples of Specific Actions	Correlating Cornerstones
Establish and maintain integrity	• Make ethical decisions, particularly as they relate to aspects of work that affect people • Demonstrate morals that illustrate your character	Trust

Trust-Building Behavior	Examples of Specific Actions	Correlating Cornerstones
Keep promises, commitments, and agreements (including implicit ones)	• If you tell someone you'll look into something, do so with vigor and keep the person updated • Recognize how others may view what you say, particularly if they perceive it as a promise	All Engagement Behaviors
Perform your responsibilities and duties competently	• Keep updated on your technical knowledge and skills through continual learning • Seek feedback from others on ways to grow in your competence	People-Centric Approach
Communicate information openly and honestly with transparency	• Share your thoughts and feelings frequently • Ask others for honest feedback	All
Consider everyone as equal partners, listening to and valuing them	• Do not always have "the answer"; sometimes ask "the question" • Use non-power oriented language when describing reporting relationships	Trust
Focus on shared goals and cooperation by asking for assistance	• Ask people to share their unique areas of expertise and experiences	Motivation
Share concern for others by doing what is right, regardless of personal risk	• Stick up for a person who may have performed in a less-than-ideal manner on an assignment you delegated to him or her	Trust
Show confidence in others' abilities and express gratitude	• Take time to provide genuine "thank you's" for work well-done • Demonstrate confidence through appropriate delegation	People-Centric Approach
Share your own thoughts, feelings, and rationales for decisions	• Explicitly share your feelings about things and explain why	Engaging Emotions
Exude warmth	• When saying "good morning," genuinely mean it • Express genuine interest in others' families and outside interests	Engaging Emotions

Trust-Building Behavior	Examples of Specific Actions	Correlating Cornerstones
Give praise to elevate others' self-esteem and confidence	• If you see a person performing well, take the time to acknowledge it • Recognize others' needs to enhance or maintain their self-esteem and take intentional actions to support them	People-Centric Approach
Accept people for who they are and appreciate their uniqueness	• Listen carefully to what people say and what they mean • Do not try to change people or convince them to be someone they are not; instead, enjoy who they are	People-Centric Approach
Appreciate and demonstrate a willingness toward mutual influence	• Be willing to allow others the chance to strongly influence or even take ownership for important assignments	Trust
Admit mistakes	• Share your own "lessons learned" when things go less-than-ideal • Openly discuss stories and previous experiences where things went less-than-ideal and how you've learned from them	People-Centric Approach

Of course, behaving in opposite ways perpetuates distrust. Additional behaviors that can create distrust include:

■ Sending mixed messages by acting and speaking inconsistently

■ Seeking personal gain rather than shared gain

■ Withholding information

■ Avoiding responsibility

■ Blaming others or making excuses

■ Jumping to conclusions

■ Micromanaging or excessive monitoring

■ Incongruence between stated values and subsequent actions.

When leaders demonstrate trust-building behaviors inconsistently, some perceive simply a flawed form of trust-building, but others perceive trust-breaking. Sometimes leaders act one way with certain people and differently with others. For example, leaders who fully disclose information with some team members yet do not share the same information with other team members are acting inconsistently. This inconsistency can lead to questions about their directness and honesty, or to concerns about whether they are withholding valuable information.

Another example of inconsistency occurs when leaders scrutinize the work of only certain individuals. Without a reasonable explanation, this kind of inconsistency can lead to questions about the leaders' integrity.

Because trust is a critical foundation of engagement, engaging leaders need to work proactively to build trust. Leaders are role models that others look toward when committing to trust-building efforts.

Trusting relationships are built one at a time. The first step is to empathize with other perspectives. Think about how others might perceive your behavior. Intentionally spend a few minutes thinking about your relationships, and try to understand what trust means to those working with and around you. Initiate explicit conversations about trust. Begin by telling others that your goal is to build a trusting relationship with them, and then ask what you can do to accomplish that goal.

■ ■ ■ ■ ■ **PRACTICE TOOL**
People-Watching

Have you ever sat in a coffee shop or shopping mall and just watched people? Observing people to identify and learn about trust- and distrust-oriented behaviors can be an interesting experiment. Take a few minutes at any location—a restaurant, a shopping mall, or even around the office—to intentionally watch for trust- or distrust-related behavioral cues.

Specifically look at peoples' body language. Body language speaks volumes about individual levels of comfort and trust:

 When a person opens or crosses his or her arms, open tends to be more trusting while crossed tends to be more guarded.

 When a person makes direct eye contact or looks away, direct eye contact tends to indicate more trust and comfort, while constantly looking away may be a sign of discomfort.

 When a person smiles or behaves stoically, smiling is a sign of comfort and connectedness, while stoic behavior may be signaling a person being guarded.

 When a person stands close to the person or farther away, allowing a person into one's "personal space" may be a signal of comfort, while putting or maintaining distance can be a sign of discomfort.

As you watch peoples' body language, ask yourself what they might be communicating non-verbally about their level of comfort and trust. And ask how this might affect your interaction with them.

The goal of observing people this way is not to make sweeping assumptions about their levels of trust or distrust. It is simply a method of recognizing trust- and distrust-oriented behaviors in action. Becoming effective at noticing behavioral cues associated with trust and distrust can help you more effectively manage your interactions with others, as observing behavioral cues can precipitate appropriate trust-building actions. When you notice a person become uncomfortable or demonstrate behaviors that may signal distrust, you can take action to explore why the person is feeling that way.

■ ■ Trust at the Speed of Conversation

In his book *Blink*,[2] Malcolm Gladwell highlights some peoples' ability to "thin-slice"—to form an immediate opinion or reaction to something based on information from our deep conscious and subconscious experiences. Given just a small amount of time or information, some individuals have the ability to make instantaneous mental notes and subsequent decisions about others and about situations. These people can almost sense things about others. Something deep within, beyond conscious thoughts, makes this possible. If individuals do have the ability to thin-slice, what are the implications for trust and engaging leadership?

How can engaging leaders build and reciprocate trust in just a few moments? How can they demonstrate trust-building behaviors convincing enough for those people thin-slicing them? Engaging leaders must learn to build trust at the speed of conversation. During conversation, it is important to read body language, judge vocal tone, and interpret other communication signals that demonstrate trust levels. Then take appropriate action by adjusting personal behaviors and words to begin building a trusting connection. This creates connections at the speed of conversation.

■ ■ ■ ■ ■ PRACTICE TOOL
Building Trust at the Speed of Conversation

It takes practice to become better at building trust at the speed of conversation. Practicing the following actions can develop your ability to more effectively build trust in a speedy manner:

Watch body language and listen to vocal tone (see the people-watching practice tool). Vocal tone, including a person's pitch and the speed of words, can say a lot about his or her level of trust. When people get nervous or lack trust they may either talk very fast or not say much at all. Or, in addition to an unusual speed, the person may have an increased pitch in voice. Both vocal tone and pitch can be good indicators that you may need to build rapport and trust quickly.

Truly listen to what people are (and are not) saying. Instead of making assumptions, listen deeply before talking and ask clarifying questions. Paraphrase, reframe, or otherwise check your understanding of what the person is saying. In cases when individuals are not voluntarily speaking, it may be necessary to inquire and ask questions to get a better sense of their comfort and trust.

Asking questions is one of the best trust-building behaviors. In particular, asking others for their opinion demonstrates that you value their perspective, which is a sign of benevolence.

If you sense someone is withholding information, ask questions to elicit information about what they are *not* saying:

- What would you do differently?

- What other considerations are there?

- What might I be missing in my thinking?

- Are there other ways to look at the situation?

- What do you think?

Demonstrate care, compassion, and understanding. When authentic, this is typically perceived as a sign of integrity and trustworthiness. Be open and candidly share your thoughts and feelings. Follow up with others: Show them your conversations are not just one-time occurrences, but they are also part of your greater commitment to building long-term relationships.

When communicating with individuals they trust, people tend not to make assumptions or inferences. Instead, they fill in the blanks more cautiously by assuming the best, or at least by giving the benefit of the doubt. It is much easier to make assumptions and inferences—and to assume the worst—about individuals who have not earned your trust.

Conversations with trusted individuals also tend to be more detailed; we inquire to find as much information as possible before making assumptions or inferences. Conversations in untrusting relationships are not as detailed; we make fewer inquiries soliciting facts or other information, choosing instead to rely on assumptions or inferences. Our perceptions go untested and increasingly rest on inaccurate information (see the ladder of inference later in this chapter).

It is important to recognize the distinction between behavior among trusted individuals and behavior among distrusted individuals. Think about how leaders treat and react to those they trust as opposed to those they do not trust. Relationships of trust between a leader and another individual are often characterized by increased engagement by the individual. This is because leaders who trust others confide in them more, share more information openly, and seek more advice.

The leader also inquires about the individual's personal life and personal aspirations. This leads to the person feeling connected. A leader treats others—those he or she does not trust—differently, often hesitantly maintaining the relationship by focusing only on work and not the person. You can probably visualize a number of relationships like this. Now, put yourself in the role of the leader. What are you doing to build trusting relationships so that you can enjoy the benefits of engaged people?

However, note that trust-building behaviors work only when coupled with authenticity. People can thin-slice genuineness quite quickly, and they often question authenticity by wondering if others have a hidden agenda. The perception of personal risk can create barriers to trust. Leaders should always act authentically, employing transparency and communication as often as possible—critical factors in mitigating opportunities for others to guess about their intentions.

■ ■ ■ ■ ■ ■ **PRINCIPLE**

> Building a trusting relationship requires authenticity.

■ ■ Building Trust Across Generations

Today's workforce spans four generations. Never before has a workforce included so many different generations working together. To build trust across generations, leaders must recognize and work to understand how the life experiences of different groups have shaped their views about work.

The most effective leaders develop a single approach to build trust and meaningful connections with everyone, regardless of generation. However, a commonly held perception suggests that leaders should develop different approaches to work with different generations. To suggest that one generation has a set of needs and another generation has a different set of needs begets stereotyping and inconsistency. Each generation has unique qualities, and each has common assumptions about the others, but leaders working to build trust across generations have a consistent responsibility to ask questions to understand others, treat the opinions and perspectives of others with respect, recognize and take advantage of individual strengths, and treat everyone fairly.

Telling stories has long been a great way to build trust across generations. Leaders who tell stories and ask others to tell stories show that they are open to sharing personal information about themselves and their experiences, and that they are eager for others to do the same. It shows they want to hear about and care about the lives of others. Sharing and inviting stories are powerful ways to reach individuals across all generations.

■ ■ ■ ■ ■ **PRACTICE TOOL**
Building Cross-Generational Trust by Telling Stories

To use storytelling:

1. Look for specific opportunities where storytelling may foster cross-generational discussion and understanding. Identify an event to use to start, pointing out themes or elements that relate to the current situation.

2. If you have time and if it will increase your confidence, tell a practice version of the story to a trusted source. Get feedback to ensure the themes of the story align with your intentions, modifying as necessary.

3. Find an appropriate time to share the story, and recite it just as you practiced, focusing on key points and cross-generational themes.

4. You may want to ask if anyone else has a story or life experience that relates to the current challenge:

   • "Has anything like this happened to you?"

   • "What have your experiences been like?"

   • "How have you reacted to similar situations?"

Asking others for similar stories is important because it invites individuals of all generations into the discussion and it shows respect for other experiences and perspectives. Once they have shared their stories, highlight the key points and connections again. When appropriate, make an explicit point about how the topic or key messages cut across generations, stressing their relevance for everyone.

■ ■ ■ Unintentional Betrayals: Repairing a Broken Trust

No matter how hard leaders try to maintain a foundation of trust, they can on occasion unintentionally betray another person. The key word here is *unintentionally*. Leaders cannot read minds; they cannot always know when they are betraying someone. People often resist discussing betrayal because they feel hurt, or because they want to avoid making a fuss or raising an issue. Despite these tendencies, and although the feelings of betrayal are often internalized, nonverbal communication seeps through just as it does amidst distrust.

A few small, unintentional betrayals typically do not alter a relationship if leaders otherwise exhibit trust-building behaviors. However, even minor, unintentional betrayals that occur too often can begin to foster distrust. Minor betrayals may result from gossiping, back-biting, or delegating work without setting someone up to succeed. Giving responsibility for a task without commensurate authority over the process can also amount to a minor betrayal, as can ever-shifting priorities, cover-ups, and miscommunications. Like weeds in the crack of a sidewalk, if minor betrayals keep popping up again and again, they become problematic.

A lack of recognition or continued insensitivity to these betrayals exacerbates them, potentially causing a major violation of trust. According to the authors of *Trust and Betrayal in the Workplace,* Dennis and Michelle Reina, "Minor betrayals are acts that alienate people from their managers, peers, and their subordinates. These subtle betrayals seem harmless and insignificant, yet can lead to more serious hurts and account for much of the pain and resignation that people feel toward their bosses, each other, and their companies."[3] In other words, minor betrayals can add up to create feelings commensurate with major betrayal. Regardless of their magnitude, betrayals also chip away at engagement levels. Even among engaged people, minor betrayals can take their toll over time, resulting in a subsequent decrease in engagement levels.

Talking to others about trust is one of the best ways to manage unintentional betrayal. Every so often, take the time to explicitly ask others what you can do to maintain their trust. To do so may sound a bit unnatural, but its effect is powerful. It communicates the importance of mutual trust among colleagues. Asking this question creates a connection between individuals because it demonstrates transparency and care. As the foundation of engagement, facilitating trust through these types of interactions strengthens relationships and creates the conditions necessary for engagement.

Of course, when they ask questions about trust, leaders must actually listen to the responses and act accordingly. Leaders should prepare themselves for any kind of response, good and bad. Asking someone for a frank opinion can result in painful feedback, which can be difficult to hear. But feedback is necessary and leaders should seek it out whenever possible without getting defensive or angry. Trust is deeply personal; whether you agree or disagree with the feedback is irrelevant because it comes from the *real* perspective of another person. Choosing to discount or not respond to difficult feedback nearly always compounds distrust.

The Ladder of Inference

The ladder of inference (see the practice tool) provides a way of better understanding how unintentional betrayals arise and escalate. This tool helps individuals minimize their assumptions and inferences, increasing their understanding and trust of others. Engaging leaders can use the ladder of inference in two ways: (1) to recognize their own assumptions and inferences, and to recognize how those elements influence their ability to build trusting relationships; and (2) to anticipate the assumptions or inferences of others, before communicating or taking action (thereby mitigating unintentional misunderstandings if possible).

Using this tool first requires an understanding of how individuals make and act upon inferences. As part of an everyday life that generates a constant stream of observations, beliefs, and opinions, people rarely test or confirm their many internal thoughts, nor do they notice when those thoughts are unconsciously labeled as facts. People then use these "facts" to make decisions and take action—and to form conclusive impressions about others.

Acting on these conclusions, people adopt new beliefs founded on previous, untested perceptions or beliefs. This process compounds on itself and becomes a reflexive loop that determines and reinforces new thoughts. Once a belief is consistently reinforced and perpetuated it becomes a truth. When beliefs or assumptions go untested, they continually compound.

■ ■ ■ ■ ■ ■ **PRACTICE TOOL**

Using the Ladder of Inference to Understand an Unintentional Betrayal

The following example shows how the ladder of inference can cause a perception of betrayal to escalate into distrust. Start at the bottom of the ladder and note how Joe leaps up the ladder, perpetuating distrust.

	A decision whether to respond (and if so, how) is made ⬆	Finally, Joe says to himself, "This is completely unfair. I am going to march into my supervisor's office and tell him that this is unfair!"
	Beliefs are adopted about the data and its relationship to the individual ⬆	Joe believes that his supervisor does not talk to anyone about performance, that he just lets everything slide, and that it is hurting Joe's team.
	Data is evaluated and causally explained; conclusions are formed ⬆	Joe then thinks, "I know why this is happening: I missed one deadline, and now I am being penalized for it. I was only late because Erica's team didn't get me the necessary information. It wasn't really my fault. My supervisor thinks it's easier to take away my work than to tell Erica's team they are messing things up."
	Data is translated; its meanings are established and labeled ⬆	Joe translates the information, "My supervisor is suggesting that my work is not up to par, and now he is taking some of my work away. He is taking my job away from me."
	Specific data or information is selected ⬆	Joe thinks to himself, "My supervisor thinks I am working slowly, and he is giving some of my work to someone else."
Start Here:	**Data or experiences are directly observed**	Joe's supervisor approaches him and says, "Joe, you are really doing an outstanding job, but your workload is slowing you down. I'm going to give some of your work to Donna."

It is important for leaders to recognize not only the behaviors that cause minor betrayals and distrust, but also how inferences and assumptions escalate into more serious betrayals and distrust. Leaders must actively prevent this from happening by recognizing situations that could potentially cause inferences to arise, initiating explicit conversations to surface assumptions, and taking action to prevent these reactions when possible.

■ ■ ■ ■ ■ **PRACTICE TOOL**
Repairing a Broken Trust

Even with the best intentions, everyone occasionally breaks trust. To maintain high levels of engagement, it is critical to repair the trust immediately. The following steps can help begin that process:

1. Take immediate action by observing and acknowledging what has happened. Proactively raise the issue by asking the person to talk about the situation.

2. During the conversation, describe your feelings and try to help the person feel comfortable talking about their own feelings. Let them vent and listen carefully. Try to understand their perspective.

3. Apologize and explain your intentions, without justifying or defending them. Always be authentic and genuine. Broken trust usually heightens our awareness of others' authenticity, and the person whose trust you broke will undoubtedly thin-slice the situation to determine your genuineness.

4. Take responsibility for your actions and hold yourself accountable as necessary. Try to explore individual contributions to the situation, but only if the other person is willing to participate: Do not force the issue. Any attempt to control or manipulate the conversation may be interpreted negatively.

5. Move forward by sharing what you have learned. Describe your plans to proactively work toward rebuilding trust.

6. If your trust was broken too, forgive them completely for the situation to move forward productively.

7. Finally, agree and reaffirm expectations for the future, expressing commitment to their priorities and to the relationship. From this point forward, make an effort to demonstrate trust-building behaviors and to maintain your commitments, checking in periodically as necessary.

■ ■ ■ Trust in Relation to the Other Cornerstones

As Warren Buffet says, "It takes twenty years to build trust and one minute to break it." Every interaction provides an opportunity to build—or break—trust. Trust is the foundation of engaging leadership and is fundamentally linked to the other cornerstones. Without genuine trust, individuals will not fully discuss their motivations, they will not believe in the benevolence of engagement nor the efficacy of having a people-centric approach to managing performance, and they will not open their minds to emotional engagement.

Without trust, the engaging leader approach is all but impossible.

ENDNOTES

1. Stephen M.R. Covey, *The SPEED of Trust: The One Thing that Changes Everything* (New York: Free Press, 2006).
2. Malcolm Gladwell, *Blink: The Power of Thinking without Thinking* (New York: Little, Brown and Company, 2005).
3. Dennis Reina and Michelle Reina, *Trust and Betrayal in the Workplace: Building Effective Relationships in Your Organization*, 2nd ed. (San Francisco: Berrett-Koehler Publishers, 2006).

3 Unique and Personal Motivators

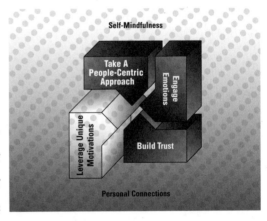

Not many people sit around thinking, "I don't want to contribute or perform my job well today." Nor is it common to find someone who doesn't want to feel good about themselves. Most people feel good when they are trusted with an important assignment that incorporates their ideas, or when they feel valued and complimented. People have a natural inclination toward motivation. As an innate human need, motivation is an important cornerstone of the engaging leader approach. Motivating others inspires their passion and excitement toward their work.

Traditional thinking about motivation suggests using control, fear, or money. Traditional top-down, control-oriented leadership prevents people from realizing their potential, and is primarily a means of achieving compliance. To access important motivators, leaders need to move away from traditional management and shift into an engaging leadership mode.

To engage others in their work, leaders should find out what gets an individual excited and what he or she feels passionate about, and then connect those elements to the person's work. Leaders should inspire others to find personally compelling reasons to *want* to engage and contribute their discretionary effort. Engaging today's workforce means stimulating individuals' key intrinsic motivators: a sense of pride, ownership, and passion for their work.

■ ■ ■ ■ ■ ■ **PRINCIPLE**

> A sense of pride, ownership, and passion for your work are
> key intrinsic motivators.

■ ■ ■ Intrinsic and Extrinsic Motivators

Intrinsic motivators compel someone to do something regardless of monetary bonuses or plaques. Instead, these motivators reward people inherently because they are in sync with personal interests, goals, needs, or desires. Examples include happiness, camaraderie with others, or wellness.

Truly engaging environments do not force superficial motivations upon people. Instead, engaging leaders create conditions that facilitate self-motivation. Forcing motivation is like pulling the strings of a puppet; facilitating self-motivation is more like coaching—helping individuals take responsibility for their own motivation. By demonstrating personal attention and interest, engaging leaders generate trust and respect, and thereby create opportunities that inspire intrinsic motivation in others.

Even while inspiring intrinsic motivation, leaders must also be prepared to provide extrinsic motivators to reward individuals for accomplishing a specific task, assignment, or mission. These extrinsic motivators include money, recognition, or other tangible benefits associated with accomplishment. Financial rewards are particularly powerful in the 21st century, as many (but not all) people equate their self-value with their income. Because individuals believe these extrinsic motivators should reflect their contributions, receiving an award is interpreted as a demonstration of personal interest in and gratitude for their efforts.

Individuals need both intrinsic and extrinsic inspiration to different degrees. The only reliable way for a leader to determine the degree to which individuals need each type of motivation is to discuss and explore motivators on an individual basis.

■ ■ ■ ■ ■ ■ **PRINCIPLE**

Engaging leaders help others accept ownership and responsibility for motivating themselves.

■ ■ ■ Digging for Gold: Searching for Individual Motivators

One of the most difficult challenges facing leaders today is uncovering what drives individuals. It is particularly challenging when the individuals themselves find it difficult to articulate their own motivators. As a result, discovering individual motivators is like discovering gold: It is difficult, but it can be very rewarding.

Different individuals have different motivators; while there are many common themes, each person is unique. A trusting interpersonal relationship with an engaging leader is essential when someone has difficulty articulating their own motivators. Without trust, individuals may find it difficult or awkward to explore these topics openly and honestly.

Empathy is the most important quality engaging leaders can demonstrate in exploring the motivations of others. Reflecting on their own experiences, leaders will likely recognize their appreciation when others took interest in their motivations. This empathetic perspective can serve as a catalyst for leaders to take action. The process of figuring out what motivates others begins during the hiring interview: Asking questions and listening for responses during an interview can lay the foundation for future conversations about motivation.

One challenge in discovering individual motivators stems from particular predispositions toward motivation. For example, many leaders fail to make time to discuss motivators because they simply expect people to automatically show up every day feeling motivated to work. And even enthusiastic leaders may tire of the extra work needed to hold these conversations. The most important thing is that these conversations happen.

Some leaders may worry that asking others what motivates them is too personal. In fact, not asking presents a greater risk. Asking a person about his or her motivations demonstrates care and respect for the person. Leaders who build trust and have good intentions are already halfway toward understanding individual motivations. The next step is to get to know and understand people as individuals.

■ ■ Recognize Who They Really Are

Engaging leaders find value in each person because they have the right intentions. Everyone matters, and everyone is important. Part of motivating others is accepting them for who they *really* are. When we see others as who we want them to be by projecting our perceptions, realities, values, and biases upon them, we do them—and ourselves—a disservice. Even though testing others against our own mental models and experiences is a normal part of being human, for leaders it can have unfortunate effects. Leaders especially must recognize people for who they really are as individuals, looking at each person's unique, individual characteristics and strengths.

Like painters looking at their palette of colors and seeing opportunities in every hue, leaders should look at the palette of individuals—each with their own hue—working with them. It may not be possible to engage each person in the same way, but it is important to recognize that everyone can add value. The greatest artists look at a color, recognize all its attributes, and use it in combination with other colors to create something magical. Colors evolve and change to maximize their potential, but their essence remains the same. Leaders should take the same approach with people, facilitating the development of individual potential.

Traditional thinking instructs leaders to treat everyone the same way. Indeed, in some cases it is unfair to treat individuals differently, not only for ethical reasons, but also because of laws mandating equality in the workplace. But each person is unique: They do not all think, work, process information, or react to work and life in the same way. These differences require leaders to individualize and personalize the way they work with others.

Attempting to change individuals to fit a single mold only complicates working relationships. Instead of changing the core of the person—who they really are—leaders must find ways to maximize their unique strengths and thereby enable them to achieve their potential.

Unfortunately, too many leaders try to change individuals instead of appreciating their unique characteristics. Even well-intentioned attempts to influence individual motivators will ultimately fail if they are based on assumptions. If a leader doesn't take the time to ask or understand what motivates an individual, the leader's assumptions may be wrong, which will likely have a negative effect on relationships.

■ ■ ■ ■ ■ ■ PRINCIPLE

People do not change easily. Get to know them as the individuals they are, not as you want them to be.

Motivating individuals requires personalizing relationships. Treating individuals differently to motivate them means creating engaging conditions for each person. Most people will like and accept a personal, customized motivation plan that meets their specific situation.

Some leaders have large teams and may find it daunting to personalize every individual relationship. Getting to know others does not happen all at once or with a single team-building session. It is undoubtedly an investment of time. But like any good investment, the return can be well worth it.

■■■■■■■■■■

> "The task of leadership is not to put greatness into people, but to elicit it, for the greatness is there already."
>
> — JOHN BUCHAN, NOVELIST AND POLITICIAN

■■■■■■■■■■

■■ Talk about Motivation

One way engaging leaders can find out what motivates others is to explicitly discuss motivation. This may sound obvious, but try to remember the last time a leader talked to you about your motivation. Most people assume they know what motivates others, using bits of information to reinforce their own assumptions, values, and biases. All subsequent interactions are then based on those assumptions rather than on real, mutually discussed individual motivators.

A Story about Assuming Motivators

I remember a young woman in a class I taught once. We were discussing how to build high-performance teams and the differences in extrinsic and intrinsic motivators among individuals. She said, "I recently got a promotion. I am new to management. In fact, I am the first person in my family to ever be in a management role."

Of course, everyone in the class was excited and proud of her. At the time I thought to myself, "Wow, she must really want to be a manager. Her motivations stem from a desire to pave a new career path for herself, to be the first manager in her family, and to have that position title."

As we continued our class conversation, though, I realized my perceptions were not quite right. Part of the story was missing. I inquired further by asking, "Maria, what is it that gets you up every morning and makes you *want* to be a manager?" She stopped for a moment, slowly smiled, and said, "Well, I am single mother with a five-year-old daughter. Even though nobody else in my family has done much with themselves, I want my daughter to know that she can grow beyond her current place in life. With the extra money I make from being a manager, I am able to save money for her so that one day she might be able to go to college. I never wanted to be a manager, but I want my daughter to know that she can take risks in life, too. Actually, that is also why I am in this class. So she can see that school is important."

Maria is a remarkable woman and her answer does not surprise me. What surprises me is that initially, I did not really understand how her internal motivators shaped her perspective. Without further exploration, I would have never known about her compelling motivators. Without testing my assumptions by asking more questions, I would have never known her unspoken, deeply rooted inspiration. Nor would I have ever known who she really is or how I could help her make the most of her desire to contribute. I would have tried motivating her using all the wrong approaches.

Recognizing the unique characteristics of others begins with genuine conversations that explicitly and openly discuss motivation. From there, leaders must listen to what is—and is not—said, willingly ask questions to understand other perspectives, glean information by monitoring individual ups and downs, and follow up with open conversations. Reactions to recognition, compensation, new assignments, work with new clients or customers, access to higher-ups, and thank you messages can all provide important information about an individual. After making observations, follow up with the individual to describe your perceptions. This discussion will provide you an opportunity to test your inferences and assumptions through discussion and dialogue.

■ ■ ■ ■ ■ ■ PRINCIPLE

Do not make assumptions about individual motivators. Instead, have explicit conversations with others about their motivation.

Because each individual is different, there is no single, magical formula for having effective conversations about personal motivators. Each conversation does, however, require that the leader show genuine interest in the individual and be willing to listen and ask reflective questions.

■ ■ ■ ■ ■ **PRACTICE TOOL**
Conversation-Starters for Discussions about Motivation

What do you know about what motivates those around you? The following conversation-starters will help initiate discussions about motivation:

☐ What are you passionate about?

☐ Tell me how you got into this position.

☐ What values drive you?

☐ If you could do anything, what would it be and why?

☐ What gets you excited?

☐ Who do you respect the most? Why?

☐ Who has had the most influence in your life?

☐ What do you believe are your best work-related skills?

☐ What do you like the best about your job?

☐ What things would you change if you could?

☐ What work-related tasks are most challenging for you?

☐ What work-related challenges would you like to conquer? Why?

☐ How can you maximize your potential today?

Individuals constantly give off clues about their motivators. A simple way to understand their motivators is the "what-why" approach. When someone makes a statement—either with words, body language, or vocal tone—simply ask, "What do you like (or not like) about this situation? Why?" With the first part of the question the leader aims to understand the situation: the context, the individuals and tasks involved, and other situational factors. By asking why, the leader seeks to understand personal preferences, desires, and motivators.

For example, "Abby, what do you like (or not like) about calling customers all day?" When Abby replies, follow up by asking "Why do you feel that way?" By asking why, you can get to the heart of the matter and not feel compelled to make an assumption or inference. Abby can explain her own feelings in her own words.

▨ ▨ View Every Interaction as an Opportunity to Motivate

Every interactive moment provides an opportunity to get to know people as individuals and to understand their motivations. But leaders often do not know what to look for, or when they see something, they brush it aside or make an assumption.

■ ■ ■ ■ ■ ▨ **PRINCIPLE**

Every interaction is an opportunity to understand others' unique motivators.

How does a leader pick up on individuals' cues and interpret conversations? Figure 3-1 offers some comments individuals often make that raise red flags about their lack of motivation—and their unspoken requests for help.

FIGURE 3-1   "Motivate Me!"

When a Person Says:	They Mean:
"How would I do that?"	Empower me to find a way to do this.
"I've tried that before."	I did not have a good experience.
"I don't have the time."	I don't see the value of this in relation to my job.
"I don't know if I can do it."	I need someone to express confidence in me.
"I'm hopeless."	I need someone to believe in me.
"I'm retiring soon."	Help me see why this is still important to me.
"Great idea, but it's not practical."	Empower me to find a way to make it practical.
"It's not my problem. It's not my job."	I don't have a personal reason to get involved.
"I've always done it this way."	Coach me with compelling reasons that make it okay to change.

■ ■ ■ Engaging Someone Who Appears Not to Care

It can be difficult to motivate someone when they do not care about their work, or when they are just biding their time until they retire. Actively disengaged people and even non-engaged individuals can sometimes behave in ways that appear to demonstrate a lack of care for their work or organization.

Engaging leaders should not buy into this assumption, but should instead take advantage of opportunities to understand and connect with people who appear not to care. Instead of keeping their guard up and turning assumptions into self-fulfilling prophesies, leaders should take the opportunity to discover how individuals truly feel. Breakthrough moments do not always occur during initial conversations, and it takes work to build and maintain constructive relationships. Engaging leaders should respond to those who appear not to care with an increased commitment to uncover and understand their motivators.

■ ■ ■ ■ ■ ■   **PRACTICE TOOL**
Engaging Someone Who Appears Not to Care

The following steps can help in conversations with individuals who appear not to care:

▪ Check your intentions. Do not have a conversation to pass judgment; have it to help the individual. Believe in your intention to help.

▪ Ask the individual if they are willing to discuss their motivation with you.

▪ State any assumptions about motivators and where they originated. Describe behaviors you witnessed that support your claim. Focus on the behaviors rather than the individual.

▪ State your reasons for initiating the conversation, which is likely to test your assumptions and offer more support.

▪ Continue asking open-ended, follow-up questions, working to inspire the individual to talk.

Here's a sample conversation:

Leader: Hi, Allejandro. I'd like to schedule some time to talk with you about motivation and what we can both do to make this year a good one. When is a good time for you?

Allejandro: I am available later this afternoon. Can we talk at 2 p.m.?

Leader: Yes, that works.

Later, at 2 p.m.

Leader: I want to talk with you about something I've noticed. It's not a fact, it's just my perception right now, but I want to talk with you about it. Is that okay?

Allejandro: Yeah, that's fine.

Leader: It appears to me that you aren't tuned into your work, that you are not as excited about it as you once were. Let me explain what behaviors I've witnessed that have led to this perception. First, I noticed that you haven't been volunteering for any assignments over the past few months. I've also seen you roll your eyes a few times during meetings when other people are talking. We recently talked about the quality of your work on a few assignments and how it hasn't met expectations. I share this with you not to call you out or make you feel uncomfortable; rather, I want to test my perception by talking with you. It appears to me that you aren't feeling excited and that you have checked out of your work. What do you think about what I've said?

Allejandro: I am not sure what to say.

Leader: Well, let's start by focusing on some of the specific behaviors I mentioned. What do you think about those? Please, let's talk honestly and specifically.

Allejandro: I guess, to be honest, you are right. I haven't been all that excited lately.

Leader: What can you tell me about that?

Allejandro: I guess I feel like I haven't been getting any exciting assignments. I know that the other team members are doing well, and they deserve the good assignments. But I think it turned me off and I just started to tune out. That, and given some personal things at home, I've been increasingly frustrated. I think all of these reasons have caused me to disconnect.

Leader: Allejandro, I really appreciate you sharing this with me. What else has been contributing to the way you are feeling?

Allejandro continues to explain his frustrations.

Leader: Let me ask you this: What can I do as your supervisor to help support you, both at work and at home? What can I do to help you get excited about work again?

The most difficult part of this conversation is initiating it. After you express your intentions, it becomes easier. While it may be an awkward conversation, reaching out and demonstrating care for the individual's disengagement is a trust-building behavior in and of itself, and it is an effective way to discover unique motivators. The key to these conversations is to have them as soon as it appears that someone does not care about what they are doing. The longer a leader waits, the more disengaged the individual may become.

Beyond having the conversation and initiating it early, keep in mind that asking what you can do to support someone works magically. Just saying, "What can I do to support you?" not only builds trust and rapport, but it also demonstrates care and support. Keeping this question open-ended allows you to choose from a variety of support approaches and mechanisms, depending on the individual's response. It also encourages the individual you are asking to take ownership by articulating and describing their own needs. This is an important element of the engaging leader approach and the relationships it helps develop: Engaging leaders accept ownership for connecting with and supporting others, and they work to help others accept ownership for their own engagement.

Individual motivators—intrinsic and extrinsic—are deeply personal. Individuals want to be motivated, challenged, and their efforts appreciated. Engaging leaders must uncover motivators through dialogue and discussion, and then seek out opportunities to use that information to motivate individuals. Even when it is difficult to match unique motivators directly to an individual's work, the individual is more likely to leverage his or her discretionary effort to be successful in the position. This requires authentic leaders who employ a personal touch to leveraging unique motivators in a way that demonstrates good intentions, trust, and genuine care.

RECOMMENDED READING

Baldoni, John. *Great Motivation Secrets of Great Leaders.* New York: McGraw-Hill, 2005.

Thomas, Kenneth W. *Intrinsic Motivation at Work: Building Energy and Commitment.* San Francisco: Berrett-Koehler Publishers, 2006.

4 A People-Centric Focus on Performance

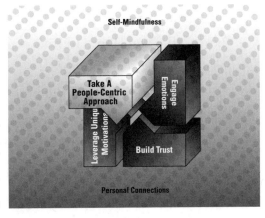

At the heart of the engaging leader approach is creating win-win situations for everyone: for the people being engaged, for the leaders themselves, and for their organizations. Engaging leadership elicits the best work from people in meaningful ways. Beyond creating conditions for engaged performance by building trust and finding unique motivators for individuals, it is important to understand how to *manage* that performance. This brings us the third cornerstone of engaging leadership: a people-centric approach to managing performance.

Increasingly over the past two decades, organizations and leaders have realized the value of systems, structures, and processes that focus on managing performance. As a result, leaders have focused on writing and aligning effective goals and then cascading those goals down to others. The use of SMART (specific, measurable, aggressive yet attainable, relevant, and time-bound) goals has become a common practice. These performance-oriented constructs allow leaders to express their expectations more effectively, which builds a more constructive working environment for everyone.

Unfortunately, many people focus so much energy on writing SMART goal statements about *what* they want to accomplish that they forget to balance their thoughts and include *how* the work will actually be accomplished. This is why engaging leaders must focus on the way they manage performance. Managing performance for increased engagement needs to be a people-centric approach that provides opportunities for others to find personally meaningful ways to engage in their work.

Leaders must recognize the past decades of workplace culture and the continuing evolution of today's workplace: For the modern employee, work is not simply about formulating and accomplishing goals. People have different expectations for the work they do. They want to accomplish their goals in a way that is meaningful to them. People want to be engaged as significant participants—almost as partners— in important processes.

This evolving perspective has serious implications for leaders trying to create an engaging workplace. They must look at performance from the perspectives of others, empathize with them, and tailor their leadership methods accordingly. Empathy means relating to and understanding the circumstances, feelings, thoughts, and needs of others, and the most effective and engaging leaders recognize how important empathy is in relationships.

■ ■ ■ ■ ■ ■ **PRINCIPLE**

> Demonstrating empathy while managing performance is the first step to a more people-centric approach.

To increase engagement, leaders must take a more people-centric, empathetic approach to managing performance. To understand why this is important, leaders can ask themselves where the most passionate, connected work comes from. Does it come from managers asking others to "jump" just because they say so? Or does it come from individuals who feel valued and involved because their managers share opportunities for influence? The great majority of those responding to this question will say that empowering others with a shared sense of control is much more likely to compel performance. A people-centric approach makes sharing control and influence a centerpiece of managing performance.

Existing performance management systems are often supervisor-centric, with supervisors telling others what to do, how to do it, and when to do it. Even those leaders with good intentions tend to maintain a significant level of control or influence over their employees' tasks and their methods for accomplishing those tasks. A *perception* of involvement may exist, but the involvement is only partially realized. Of course, allowing individuals to make *all* the decisions about their work is usually an unbalanced approach as well.

Taking a more people-centric approach involves shifting our paradigm of leadership roles. Instead of being autocratic or control-oriented, leadership must be considered a source of empowerment. The focus moves from what you want to what individuals want. Leaders' roles then shift slightly in that they now have responsibility to ensure that what individuals want also benefits the team and the organization. A people-centric approach mutually satisfies individuals, leaders, and their organizations.

Figure 4-1 depicts the difference in how work is viewed. In the manager-centric approach the manager plays a more directive role by telling people what to do and how to do it. In a people-centric approach, the manager focuses on collaborating with individuals to involve them in ways that are meaningful to those individuals.

How do leaders develop a more engaging, people-centric approach to their work? Engaging leaders involve others in decisions, provide clear and appropriate assignments, discuss performance often, leverage individual strengths, and provide recognition.

FIGURE 4-1   Manager- vs. People-Centric Approaches

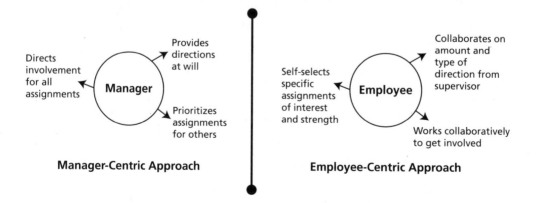

▪ ▪ ▪ Involve Others in Decisions

One of the most valued aspects of becoming an adult and a working professional is our influence in making decisions. While many people are willing to pay their dues and work up the typical ladder of authority, they always want some level of influence over certain portions of their work. (Of course, certain facets of work, like rewriting a job description, are not as open to personal control as others.) Engaging leaders find appropriate ways to intentionally involve people in decisions that affect them.

▪ ▪ ▪ ▪ ▪ ▪ PRINCIPLE

Engaging leaders find ways to intentionally involve people in decisions that affect them.

So how do engaging leaders provide others with a greater sense of involvement and decision-making? First and foremost, engaging leaders ask others for their opinions. Nothing makes an individual feel quite as valued as when someone asks for their opinion. Asking for an opinion suggests a respect for their ability to think and make contributions based on their own valuable, unique experiences.

Leaders themselves have different needs and interests when it comes to influence and control. Involving others in decisions requires a willingness to let go of some level of control, which is not always easy. Figure 4-2 shows how leaders can consider their own interests and the interests of others, and how they can involve others in the decision-making process.

FIGURE 4-2 Involving Others in the Decision-Making Process

Individual's Desired Level of Involvement	High	Delegate to Individual	Offer Ownership to Individual
	Low	Do Not Involve Individual	Seek Advice from Individual
		Low	High
		Importance of Work to Individual	

When involving others, engaging leaders consider an individual's desired level of involvement and the importance of the work to them. Their interests can guide decisions about what level of involvement to give them. A people-centric approach empathizes with their perspective and relies on their wants and needs as the primary mechanism for making decisions about involvement. It involves explicitly discussing their perspective as often and as realistically as possible before asking them to take on a new assignment. Once again, the relationship requires balance: Involving others only when they desire it is unrealistic. Engaging leaders simply try to engage others in proportion to the way the decision affects them, but only to the extent possible.

■ ■ ■ Provide Clear and Appropriate Assignments

One day, a first-time supervisor gave John, a top-notch team member, an assignment. The assignment was to get a rock and bring it back to the supervisor. John thought to himself, "This should be no problem. I know just where to get a rock." The next morning, John eagerly approached his supervisor with a rock in hand. As he reached out to give the rock to the supervisor, the supervisor looked at it and said, "Oh, shoot, that's not the rock I had in mind. Can you get me a bigger rock?" John, a little disappointed, shrugged it off and said, "Sure, no problem." John then went out and searched for a larger rock. Upon finding one, he grinned and said, "That's it! I've got it." The next day, much to John's dismay, his supervisor once again said, "I'm sorry, John, but that's not the rock I expected you to bring back. The one I want is big and green, not gray." As you can imagine, this guessing game between the supervisor and John could have continued on and on for some time.

Ambiguous assignments can be challenging and disappointing, even for the best of employees. The more often an individual receives an ambiguous assignment, the more likely he or she is to become non-engaged. Ambiguous assignments make leaders seem like they lack concern about the time, abilities, and interests of others.

For engaging leaders, a shared understanding of mutually shared expectations is critical. Putting forth the care and energy to contribute and then finding out that the work does not meet expectations because of insufficient instructions is disheartening; what's more, it can foster resentment and frustration. If these misunderstandings continue to occur over time, the frustration may continue grow and perpetuate disengagement.

It is critical for engaging leaders to provide a description of the context of an assignment. Discuss the factors that make the assignment important and the specific roles involved in accomplishing the assignment. Giving context illustrates your trust in the individual and can be the primer for establishing shared understanding of shared expectations.

■ ■ Developmental Assignments Increase Engagement

Engaging others through performance requires delegating developmentally appropriate assignments. Leaders too often hastily delegate an assignment and rationalize it as a "good experience," regardless of what it requires to be successful. What a rationale! Would you let your doctor say that about surgery? "Well, Joe, it looks like we may want to do a spinal tap. That'll provide some good training experience for our nurses." That would come across as ridiculous. Similarly, leaders need to give thought to assignments they delegate. Like a doctor prescribing the best procedure, a good diagnosis of individual readiness is critical, and this involves some customizing for individuals.

Engaging leaders should aware of the assignments they delegate, intentionally providing interesting and developmental assignments to those who desire them. To some, interesting assignments are like the oxygen a fire needs to maintain its strength: A fire can last for some time with just a small amount of oxygen, but over time it diminishes or dies without it. Maintaining individual levels of engagement requires opportunities to add oxygen to their internal fires. And while not every work environment offers the luxury to pick and choose assignments, some level of discretion is usually available.

It is not a new concept for leaders and managers to offer assignments that provide opportunities to stretch individual thinking and knowledge by learning something new or taking on new role—commonly known as *stretch* assignments. Engaging leaders must intentionally and thoughtfully create these opportunities for others. Try not to focus on the outcome of the assignment, but on *how* the assignment is ultimately accomplished. After all, engaging others by providing new assignments may mean accepting more mistakes or lower-quality performances initially. The experience has two goals in mind: (1) to provide appropriate and interesting work for the individual; and (2) to demonstrate that the leader cares about—and is willing to take a chance on—the individual's growth and development.

When considering a stretch assignment for someone, it is also important to consider their strengths and interests. Individuals tend to become more engaged as their assignments become more interesting and opportunities to leverage their strengths increase. Recall for a moment an assignment delegated to you that allowed you to leverage your particular strengths to create a successful outcome and make a contribution. How exciting and empowering was it to have someone ask you—given your special knowledge, skills, and abilities—to complete that assignment? Leaders who work to create more stretch assignments are more likely to see an increase in individual engagement.

Appropriate assignments enhance engagement because they reveal leaders who know and appreciate the strengths and interests of others, and who use their understanding of individuals' unique abilities to positively impact those individuals and the entire organization. This requires leaders to truly know the individuals working around them, and to intentionally use their unique skills and abilities as appropriate. When leaders delegate enjoyable assignments that are challenging and developmental, individuals recognize their leaders' efforts to look out for their best interests. Engaging leaders should also follow up with effective feedback and coaching throughout the course of the assignment.

*Jackson is approaching the completion of his year-end bud-
get cycle. Having been in this department for almost 15 years,
he knows the work like the back of his hand. But this year he
doesn't plan to do the work himself. He's been considering how
to involve Heidi. He knows that Heidi is very detail-oriented
and enjoys the meticulous process of checking and rechecking
detailed work. Therefore, he makes a conscious choice to involve Heidi in this as a stretch assignment. Although she has
not previously been responsible for an assignment of this size,
he provides her a portion of it that allows her to leverage her
attention to detail.*

The assignment in this story is important on multiple levels. First,
it shows Heidi that her leader Jackson cares about her development.
Second, it puts her in a position to succeed because she can leverage
her knowledge and strengths on an important assignment. Delegating this assignment to Heidi not only makes her feel great about the
work she's doing, but it also engages her.

■ ■ ■ Discuss Performance Often

Humans are living creatures that require certain kinds of nourishment. Engaging work environments consistently provide information
about individual performance as a way of providing nourishment—
not enough and people become malnourished, which results in a loss
of energy. Too much and our body rejects it, making us feel ill. Engaging leaders should find an amount of feedback that is just right.

Feedback is important to engagement on multiple levels. First, it requires individual accountability for both effective and ineffective behaviors. Individuals are credited with their successes, but when they do not meet expectations, their leader must provide developmental feedback and coaching to ensure future success. The two primary goals of effective feedback include differentiating good performance from poor, and emphasizing the lessons of feedback as a means to increase interest and engagement.

Leaders should always consider the quality and consistency of feedback to deliver it appropriately. Without consistent feedback, it is difficult to know whether anyone cares about what we do, or even notices. Offering specific, personalized feedback demonstrates that an engaging leader cares about individual success and is interested in helping others succeed—another sign of benevolence.

One way to deliver specific, behavior-focused feedback is to use the "what-what-why" approach for developmental feedback and the "what-why" approach for positive reinforcement and recognition (see Figure 4-3).

The what-what-why approach to developmental feedback describes *what* the individual has done, *what* you would recommend the individual do differently in the future, and *why* you think an alternative method would be more effective moving forward. The what-why approach to positive feedback describes *what* the individual has done and *why* their particular method was effective.

FIGURE 4-3   Approaches to Developmental Feedback

Individual Action	Your Recommendations	Why It's More Effective
Jack, I believe you pushed the group to make a decision very quickly. It seemed there was a strong focus on the task.	I think you might have checked with people to see how they felt about the decision, giving more focus to those relationships.	It may be more effective because it would probably increase acceptance of the decision and it would show others you appreciate them.

Individual Action	Why It's Effective
Janice, it was really helpful when you asked if anyone had another perspective to share.	I think it was helpful because it gave everyone a chance to offer an opinion about the situation.

Offering this type of specific feedback creates a trusting relationship because it is thorough, explicit, and caring. It also provides suggestions to help improve or maintain an individual's performance, which is often missing in feedback. Either of these examples should be followed up by asking the individual what they think about your feedback. This involves the individual and maintains a two-way conversation about their performance.

■ ■ Explicitly Learning from Performance

When individuals make mistakes or do not live up to their potential, one way to engage them is by asking them to think about what they can learn from the mistake and what they would do differently in the future. Traditional leaders often think they ask this question frequently enough, but they usually do not get to the heart of the matter, which is a genuine interest in win-win situations through open-ended discussions, real development, and future-focused engagement.

Learning lessons from less-than-ideal performances begins by asking the right questions, as opposed telling an individual they have made a mistake. Most people recognize it on their own when they make a mistake or do not live up to their potential. Coming down too hard on an individual only creates a fear-based relationship, seriously harming engagement. Instead of learning from mistakes, they will begin to fear mistakes, and the difference is significant.

Once lessons learned are out on the table, sufficient follow-up and coaching are critical to help individuals change their behavior. Do not assume that because a lesson has been explicitly discussed everyone knows what to do and will remember in the future. They may not always be held accountable the next time a similar situation arises, or they may repeat the same mistake or behavior. Engaging leaders follow up to ensure performance-related learning by understanding what has happened, planning a different behavior or reaction in the future, and working with others to practice and continue learning as new situations arise.

■ ■ Accountability and Alignment

When individuals are engaged they are passionate, committed, and energized. Accountability is an important factor in engagement that means learning from poor performance and recognizing individuals when they meet or exceed expectations. Engaging leaders hold individuals accountable because it demonstrates that their work is important and valuable.

Even highly engaged individuals should be held accountable. If not, they may have the perception that the leader does not care or is disinterested. In those cases, it is only a matter of time before highly engaged individuals lower their performance standards and their engagement diminishes. To maximize engagement, individuals must be held accountable for their work.

■ ■ ■ ■ ■ ■ **PRINCIPLE**

> For maximum engagement, individuals must be held accountable for their work. Accountability demonstrates that an individual's work is important.

Accountability also means aligning work with the mission and goals of the organization. Engaging leaders should draw clear lines directly from any task or assignment to team, division, and organization goals. Similarly, an organization should cascade its goals down to each individual with clarity and describe how individual work contributes to the organization.

Figure 4-4 shows how cascading goals trickle down from the organizational level to the individual level. An individual should be able to draw a clear line from anything he or she does and tie it directly to organizational goals.

FIGURE 4-4   Cascading Goals

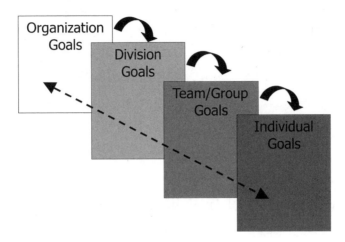

Aligning performance to organizational goals provides a view of where individual work fits into the greater system.

■ ■ ■ Leverage Individual Strengths

Engaging leadership means recognizing the unique strengths and talents of individuals. Individuals are much more capable of enhancing their natural skills and abilities than they are of fixing their weaknesses. The world of sports provides countless examples of this in practice. Consider a baseball game: A specific batter is often called in during unique situations to achieve a specific result like a bunt down the third base line or a line drive into right field. Pitchers are also called in to work a left-handed batter or close a game. In these situations, coaches—the leaders of their team—leverage individual strengths to win games.

Engaging leaders systematically and consistently take advantage of individual strengths, which implies a knowledge of those strengths.

Discovering and tapping into the strengths and passions of others lays the groundwork for individuals to use their discretionary effort to accomplish extraordinary things. While many leaders know that certain individuals have certain strengths, and while they often try to tap into those strengths, traditional leadership methods too often focus on assigning tasks that either fail to showcase individual talents or that force individuals to use weaker skills. Asking individuals to work using weaker skills is like asking right-handed individuals to write with their left hand. To get the best work from others, engaging leaders must tap into the best abilities of others.

■ ■ ■ ■ ■ ■ PRINCIPLE

Engaging leaders systematically and consistently find ways to tap into individual strengths.

Leveraging individual strengths has additional benefits. Using specific strengths often facilitates the emergence of new, additional strengths. For example, if Alexis determines that strategic thinking is a strength of hers, and if she is given an additional work assignment or project that involves strategic thinking, it is highly likely that she will also develop additional skills related to strategic thinking, such as effective questioning, critical thinking, and creative thinking. Those skills will grow in and of themselves as a result of leveraging her strategic thinking skills.

While traditional approaches to leadership involve identifying and fixing weaknesses, the engaging leader approach identifies and builds on the unique strengths of individuals to enable them to reach their full potential.

▪ ▪ Not Fitting Squares into Circles

To leverage individual strengths, leaders must recognize those strengths. Individuals may or may not be aware of their own strengths, or they may have an idea of their contributions but not really understand why they are effective. Leaders may feel the same way, recognizing individual contributions without always identifying what exactly makes them special. Sometimes it is difficult to identify individual strengths because people's behaviors and actions seem to happen so naturally. Unfortunately, it is easy to overlook those strengths or take them for granted.

For example, Alice, a CFO, works with a colleague, Yolanda, who is an extremely effective critical thinker. Stepping back from given situations, Yolanda quickly considers multiple perspectives, compares and contrasts alternative options, and often comes to a clear and optimal decision. Because this appears to be a natural skill for her, Alice and other colleagues often seek out Yolanda's advice. After a while, it becomes a standard part of the way others interact with her, and it is easy to take her abilities for granted because they seem so natural. Engaging leaders make it a point to explicitly know and acknowledge individual strengths.

▪ ▪ ▪ ▪ ▪ ▪ ▪ ▪ ▪

"We all spend too much time trying to remedy our weaknesses rather than building our strengths. Knowing and facing your weaknesses *is* a strength."

— HOWARD GARDNER, PSYCHOLOGIST

■■■■■ **PRACTICE TOOL**
Four Steps in Discussions about Strengths

The following process can help you begin a discussion about individual strengths. Keep in mind that the most effective conversations and relationships are built on a foundation of trust.

1. Describe your intentions, with particular emphasis on how you plan to use the information gained from the conversation.

2. Describe your impression of the individual's particular strengths.

3. Ask for a response to your perceptions and ask if the person can name additional strengths.

4. Conclude the conversation by describing how you will follow up with the person based on your conversation, including how you hope to leverage the person's strengths in the future.

Consider the following sample conversation between Susan, an engaging leader, and her subordinate Janice for more ideas:

Susan: Hi, Janice. How are things going?

Janice: Fine, Susan. How are you?

Susan: Doing well, thanks. I am really glad we have a chance to talk. First let me tell you my thoughts and intentions for this conversation. How does that sound?

Janice: Sounds good. I was curious about what you meant when you told the team you wanted to find better ways of leveraging individual strengths.

Susan: I recognize that each person on our team has specific strengths—whether it's knowledge, experience, or skills—that allow each of you to perform exceptionally in certain areas. I want to figure out what those strengths are and provide opportunities for you to use those strengths more often. How does that sound to you?

Janice: I like it.

Susan: I've thought of a number of strengths my perspective tells me you have. I want to share those with you and then I also want to see if there are additional strengths I can add to the list. But first, I want to know what you think your strengths are.

Janice: Ok. Well, I think I am good at working with people.

Susan: That's helpful. Can you elaborate on what you mean? What kinds of personal behaviors demonstrate your ability to work well with people?

Janice: I focus on the person and try to avoid distractions. I do this because . . . (continues).

Susan: Great. I think it's my turn to share what I think your strengths are. First . . . (explains strengths). What do you think about the areas I've mentioned? Also, are there any other strengths you'd like to include?

Janice: I appreciate you sharing your impressions. I never thought of that behavior as a strength, but I guess it is. You have triggered my thinking. I also think that I am good at . . . (continues).

Susan: Now, I know that just because people are good at some things doesn't mean that they also enjoy doing those things! Heck, I am good at washing the dishes, but I hate doing it! So, of the strengths we discussed, which ones do you enjoy the most?

Janice explains her perspective.

Susan: Thank you for sharing that with me. It really helps me get to know you better. As we move forward, I want to try to find ways to incorporate your strengths into specific assignments. How does that sound to you? Do you have any questions?

Janice: I think it sounds great. But I was wondering, does this mean that we are not going to focus on my weaknesses or developmental areas?

Susan: That is a great question. We all have strengths and weaknesses. I want to try to give you assignments that use the strengths you enjoy. But there will definitely be assignments that will cause you to use other skills that you may still be developing. That is unavoidable. We will still work on developing those skills, and you will still have an opportunity to receive training in those areas. I just want to be sure to tap into your strengths and also build on them. How does that sound?

Janice: That sounds good. I am looking forward to it!

Susan: Me, too. I think that's it for now. We will definitely continue this conversation in the future. I'll also try to explicitly share with you when I am trying to take advantage of your strengths with an assignment, or when I intend for you to develop non-strengths.

Engaging leaders discover individual strengths in a number of ways. Having a simple, strengths-based conversation is a good place to begin. Those with a strong sense of their strengths are likely to easily share them with someone who asks. When discussing individual strengths, it is important for people to know with confidence that their leader is asking with good intentions and will act with benevolence.

Engaging leaders can also explore individual strengths by considering the implicit skills involved in day-to-day work. Monitor individuals over time and think about what they do well and what particular behaviors make the tasks a strength. Make a list of these—either on paper or in your head—and when new assignments come up, consider who is best positioned to use his or her strengths.

Other approaches may include reviewing individual performance appraisals, self-assessments, or evaluations like 360-degree assessments and peer feedback. Each of these can offer insights into things the individual does particularly well and that can be capitalized on. Particularly look for patterns or trends that emerge where the individual was using specific knowledge or skills that were an asset.

Leaders cannot completely ignore job aspects that are not using individual strengths, nor can they completely forget about individual weaknesses. Engaging leaders should actively strike a balance between uncovering and using individual talents and mitigating individual weaknesses.

■ ■ Caveats to Consider when Leveraging Individual Strengths

Keep in mind that individual perceptions of personal strengths may not always be realistic. For example, Tim may think of himself as an excellent golfer, and his buddies may confirm that his golf game is outstanding. But if Tim's buddies do not know a good game of golf compared to a bad game of gold, then their feedback to Tim is somewhat misleading. Tim's notion of golf as a personal strength may be incongruent with his actual abilities.

Individuals may overestimate a personal strength or they may believe they are doing one thing when in reality they are doing something else. These incongruities can provide a great starting point for leaders to coach others. When using care in doing so, and when genuinely intending to help others, leaders can build trust and enhance individual strengths.

Another important caveat to consider when leveraging individual strengths (as previously suggested) is that just because someone has talent with particular tasks does not mean that they also enjoy fulfilling those tasks. For example, Ben, a front-line manager, has a colleague, Mia, who is an excellent editor. Mia has a degree in English and an advanced degree in professional writing. But while editing is certainly a strength of hers, her job has nothing to do with editing. In fact, after completing her degrees, she determined that the world of editing and professional writing was not for her. She does not enjoy it in the way she thought she would.

If her manager, Ben, were to look myopically at Mia's strengths, he would most likely classify editing as one of them. But without further inquiry, he might not realize that she does not enjoy using that strength. This distinction is important because even though engaging leaders should leverage individual strengths, they should also try coordinate those efforts with individual preferences.

Individual strengths usually correlate with personal interests and preferences because it is comfortable to fulfill tasks that make us feel confident and talented. But this is not always the case, and leaders who leverage individual strengths without concern for personal preferences can foster disengagement. This is why a strengths-focused conversation is important.

■ ■ ■ ■ ■ ■ ■ ■ ■ ■

"Great groups become great only when everyone in them, leaders and members alike, is free to do his or her absolute best. . . . The best thing a leader can do for a great group is allow its members to discover their own greatness."

- Warren Bennis and Patricia Ward Biederman, *Organizing Genius*

▪▪▪ Provide Recognition

Engaging leaders build confidence in others, and a great way to do this is by recognizing individual contributions. Even though our work lives go by in days, weeks, and months, we really live for *moments* of contribution, value, and personal pride and fulfillment. Individuals feel valued when contributing their ideas and leveraging their own strengths to fulfill clear and specific assignments they believe in or have a vested interest in. It is important to recognize individuals for these contributions. Think of recognition like an engagement energy bar: When individuals need a jolt, engaging leaders find ways to give them genuine, honest praise and recognition. Engaging leaders know that individuals need this type of energy lift and that waiting to receive it in an annual performance appraisal is too long. The frequency of recognition needed varies among individuals, but everyone needs some fairly consistent recognition to feel valued and appreciated, and to maintain or foster engagement.

It is important for leaders to recognize the difference between offering recognition and offering *effective* recognition, even though most forms of recognition are done with good intentions. Saying something simple like "good job" is not specific enough. Effective recogni-

▪▪▪▪▪▪ PRINCIPLE

Even though our work lives go by in days, weeks, and months, we really live for *moments* of contribution, value, and personal pride and fulfillment. Consistent recognition is a primer for engagement.

tion requires explicit descriptions of what the individual has done to receive the recognition. Saying "good job" is also often ineffective because it does not adequately describe the impact of the performance. Notice the difference between the following two examples:

■ Example #1: "Good job on that assignment, Juanita."

■ Example #2: "Good job on the Newman Project, Juanita. Your detailed report allows everyone to not only see your team's progress, but it also shows us exactly where the rest of our efforts fit into the overall plan. Your suggestions for next steps provide a roadmap of our direction moving forward, which will be very helpful during the next planning stage."

Receiving recognition is a deeply personal experience. Some individuals like public recognition, while others prefer more low-key, personal praise. Recognizing others in ways that make them uncomfortable can reinforce how little you know about them, and it signifies an immaturely developed relationship. And repeated or consistent feelings of discomfort can perpetuate disengagement. Simply asking someone what kind of recognition they prefer is a good way to ensure their comfort.

■ ■ ■ ■ ■ ■ ■ ■ ■

"Everyone likes a compliment."

- ABRAHAM LINCOLN, U.S. PRESIDENT

"The deepest human need is the need to be appreciated."

— WILLIAM JAMES, PSYCHOLOGIST AND PHILOSOPHER

Keep in mind, false praise or recognition for poor performance can actually contribute to disengagement. Individuals usually know when they did not contribute their best work. If they are given false praise in such situations, they may tell themselves that it is not necessary to fully engage in their performance to receive recognition.

Star performers need encouragement, too. Leaders may not encourage these individuals as often because they usually appear self-motivated. Even though star performers usually are self-motivated, they still need recognition to maintain their efforts and to feel acknowledged and useful.

There is no single best way to offer recognition. For many, it is not the recognition itself that maintains or enhances engagement, but the feelings associated with the recognition—feelings like pride, confidence, commitment, and even hope. These emotional reactions to recognition drive others toward continued success and induce the kind of behaviors that result in future praise as well.

■ ■ ■ ■ ■   **PRACTICE TOOL**
Conversation-Starters for Discussions about Recognition

Sometimes the most difficult part of a conversation is finding a way to initiate it. Use the following conversation-starters to begin discussions about recognition.

1. Describe your intentions, with particular emphasis on how you plan to use the information gained from the conversation.

2. Start the conversation by asking one of the following questions:

   - How do you like to be recognized? In public? In private? In written or verbal format? Another way?

   - What can I do to let you know that you are appreciated?

   - Tell me about a time when you received recognition you did not appreciate. What happened?

   - What type of recognition excites you the most?

   - What type of recognition is most meaningful to you?

   - Who do you find it important to receive recognition from?

   - In your life and work experiences, what has been the greatest moment of recognition for you? Why?

3. Conclude the conversation by letting the individual know that you intend to keep their responses in mind when you recognize them for a job well done. Also let them know that you would appreciate feedback on how well you adhere to their preferences regarding recognition, and that you will follow up with additional discussions in the future.

Engaging leaders help others realize the importance of their work and how their effective performance fits into the greater work of the organization. Leaders at higher levels of the organizational structure can offer even greater impact to those they recognize. For example, Holly once recalled an experience when the director of another business unit approached her and said, "Holly, I've been hearing a lot of good things about you. Your work on the client-commissioned project has really made a difference in helping us reach our mid-year goals."

Not only was Holly surprised to learn that the director knew her personally, but she was even more surprised that the director also knew about her work. By offering a specific example of her work and describing its importance to the organization, the director fueled her internal fire enough to last for a long time. For Holly, the recognition felt really, really great.

Engaging leaders do not underestimate the power of simply recognizing individuals for their contributions. Doing so fuels positive emotions and increases engagement levels.

A Story about Recognition

At a workshop I recently attended, a facilitator told a story about the coach of a little league baseball team in Houston, Texas. After each game, the coach said something positive about each kid on the team. He found the good in each kid by recognizing their unique contributions to the team. After a few weeks of this, the team members stopped making fun of and teasing one another. Instead, they began encouraging one another and lifting up spirits when the team lost a game or an individual made a mistake on the field. This team was not the most talented in the league, but they did have the best camaraderie. And by the end of the season, they had won the city championship.

If you encourage others, they will begin believing in themselves. Once that happens, they will act like champions.

RECOMMENDED READING

Buckingham, Marcus, and Donald Clifton. *Now, Discover your Strengths.* New York: The Free Press, 2001.

Rath, Tom, and Donald O. Clifton. *How Full is Your Bucket? Positive Strategies for Work and Life.* New York: The Gallup Press, 2004.

5 The Renewable Resource of Emotion

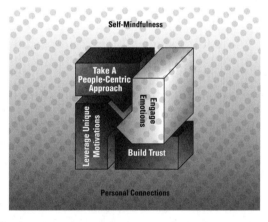

Traditional leaders have often operated analytically, choosing intellect over emotion in the workplace. This is not surprising given the industrial revolution of the 20th century and its emphasis on creating efficient processes at all costs. However, focusing wholly on what is accomplished and not on *who* is accomplishing it is a mistake that costs organizations enormous amounts of money, time, and resources through disengagement—not to mention the immeasurable toll it takes on the individuals themselves. If engaging leadership means leveraging individual discretionary effort, then it is necessary to emotionally engage people. The most engaging leaders know that emotional fuel is a renewable energy resource.

Organizational cultures often ignore and neglect individual emotional perspectives, forcing people to suppress their feelings at work. But when individuals are not engaged emotionally, how can they be engaged otherwise? How can they connect in a purely analytical way? Engaging leaders encourage emotions as part of the workplace, because they instinctually recognize that emotions drive individuals. One way to inspire others to use their discretionary effort and maximize their potential is to leverage their emotions.

■ ■ ■ Why Emotions Are Critical to Engagement

Positive emotions often create better work environments, enhance job satisfaction, improve performance, and increase engagement. Conversely, negative emotions like stress, anxiety, frustration, and anger often create toxic work environments that decrease engagement. Essentially, individuals are emotional before they are rational. Emotions play a huge role in personal satisfaction and willingness to contribute. They are not necessarily centered around the "soft stuff"—a term often used to characterize people-oriented interactions as opposed to task-oriented interactions or "hard stuff." The goal is to *align* minds with hearts to create more powerful experiences.

More often than not, individuals are emotional before they are rational. Rational commitment attracts individuals to particular organizations. In other words, individuals take jobs in organizations because of their reputation, the purpose of their work, or the associated benefits. These characteristics are attractive because they are logically or rationally compelling.

But logical reasoning does not necessarily maintain individual engagement after joining an organization. Without benevolence and

■ ■ ■ ■ ■ ■ ■ ■ ■ ■

"The soft stuff is always harder than the hard stuff."

— ROGER ENRICO, PEPSICO EXECUTIVE

■ ■ ■ ■ ■ ■ ■ ■ ■ ■

emotional appeal, individual commitment levels tend to diminish. Individual emotional commitment is a driver for using discretionary effort. In an environment offering only rational satisfaction and not emotional satisfaction, individuals eventually burn out and leave in search of emotional connections.

■ ■ ■ ■ ■ ■ PRINCIPLE

Individuals are emotional before they are rational, and emotions drive engagement.

Emotions triggered by human interactions with coworkers, colleagues, and most importantly, leaders, are more powerful and influential than purely analytical stimulation. Positive emotions drive productivity and success; negative emotions can contribute to active disengagement. The Corporate Leadership Council's research on the roles of both emotions and rational thinking in engagement[1] found that emotional engagement increases the use of individual discretionary effort at four times the rate of rational engagement. Engaging leaders create emotional connections between individuals and their work, and the possibilities that result from this are endless.

It's not that people can't be engaged both rationally and emotionally—it's just that emotional engagement is more powerful. The most compelling experiences in life are usually driven by emotions and created by feelings of hope, joy, satisfaction, and inspiration. Even people who are rationally driven or intellectually driven thrive on emotions. People who like to think rationally tend to *feel* comfort and confidence in being rational. People who are driven by intellectual thinking may thrive in situations where they can exercise their brain. The question is, how do they *feel* when they are stimulated through thinking? They likely *feel* challenged, excited, compelled or even satisfied after the thinking process. Emotional reactions seem to underlie the rational and intellectual preferences. The emotional sides of people are what drive engagement.

Traditional leadership declares rational thinking to be the best way to deliver successful performances. Modern leaders elicit successful performances by leveraging emotions; emotions almost always differentiate between average and exceptional performances.

▪ ▪ ▪ Every Interaction is an Opportunity to Engage Emotions

Every human interaction in the workplace—both positive and negative—causes individuals to react in ways that essentially compel them or dissuade them to perform. When individuals receive a new assignment, when they accept a promotion or a raise, or when someone offers them a compliment, their reaction is usually emotional. How can leaders leverage these typical emotional reactons to engage others?

Most individuals have numerous interactions with others during the course of a normal work day. This may include saying hi to someone else in the hallway, participating in a phone conference or an in-person meeting, or even sending an email or memo to someone else.

"In everyone's life, at some time, our inner fire goes out. It is then burst into flame by an encounter with another human being. We should be thankful for those people who rekindle the inner spirit."

— Albert Schweitzer, philosopher and Nobel Peace Prize winner

A Story about Engaging Emotions

In 1995, a fire destroyed Aaron Feuerstein's Malden Mills factory. The Malden Mills company makes popular Polartec® fleeces. While Feuerstein could have taken the $300 million insurance money for himself, he empathized with the company's 2,000 employees and used the money to personally pay their salaries for three months while a new factory was being rebuilt. Instead of allowing his employees to disengage and disconnect over this devastating situation, his empathy reengaged his workers. When the company was in financial straits a few years later, its employees returned the sentiment by offering to accept lower wages and work longer hours to save the company.

Every one of these interactions provides an opportunity to engage emotions.

Leaders should recognize that people do not shut off their emotional radar when they come to work. They may hide it or tuck it away, but it is always present. Therefore, every time a leader has an interaction—no matter how big or small—an individual will register an emotional perception. If a leader walks by in the hallway without acknowledging a team member's presence, he or she may be perceived as cold or lacking interest. While this may not be the leader's intention, it may be the perceptual reality of the person experiencing it.

A leader with his or her emotional radar on will recognize these moments as opportunities to build relationships, including trust, which can create emotional connections and increase engagement.

Individuals like to know when others truly know them, understand them, and care for them. Leaders should recognize that emotions and other elements of personal life contribute to the identity of others, and it is very important to demonstrate a personal understanding of those elements. Leaders should learn how to take advantage of opportunities to engage individuals emotionally.

Creating Emotional Connections

Everyone has some level of emotional connection with others, and engaging leadership can enhance these connections. Developing emotional connections with others does not happen overnight, it can be challenging and it sometimes requires individuals to change old, deeply embedded habits. For example, a traditional manager who has never discussed his feelings in the workplace—even if his feelings are work-related—may begin by explicitly sharing his feelings of joy over a recently well-done initiative. Another example is a person who is not very self-aware and may have a difficult time sensing how her emotions influence her behaviors. With a long history of this unawareness, she may have a difficult time intentionally creating emotional connections.

Individual social patterns are not only behavioral, but they are also physiologically wired in the brain over time. When someone engages someone else emotionally, they literally create new patterns of brain wiring. This happens subconsciously, but it sometimes surfaces in

■ ■ ■ ■ ■ ■ **PRINCIPLE**

We cannot separate who we are in life from who we are at work. Whole people needed to be treated like whole people, which includes their emotional self.

■ ■ ■ ■ ■ ■ ■ ■ ■

"One person with passion is better than forty people merely interested."

— E.M. FORSTER, NOVELIST, SHORT-STORY WRITER, AND ESSAYIST

■ ■ ■ ■ ■ ■ ■ ■ ■

related ways, like in a sudden loss of confidence, for example. The way individuals react to emotional situations makes up part of who they believe they are—part of their identity.

Developing emotional connections may involve changing personal conceptions of identity—an unsettling proposition for many. It is common to resist these types of changes, which makes developing emotional connections more difficult than developing purely cognitive skills. But developing emotional connections requires that individuals *want* to develop them, and we must recognize that changing personal behaviors takes time.

One of the leading models used to understand individual change readiness is the Transtheoretical Model for Change, developed by psychologists James O. Prochaska, Ph.D., and Carlo C. DiClemente, Ph.D.[2] The model identifies five stages of change and other factors that describe intentional change and common decision-making characteristics.

■ ■ ■ ■ ■   **EXERCISE**

Are You Ready for Change?

Using the five stages that organize the Transtheoretical Model for Change, the following table considers those stages as they could relate to individual willingness to emotionally connect with others in the workplace.

Level	Change Stages Correlating to Emotional Connections in the Workplace	Description
Level 1	Precontemplation	Not recognizing that you may or may not have emotional connections. Often signified by denying a need for emotional connections, or by concluding that there is not any room for improvement.
Level 2	Contemplation	Recognizing the need to develop emotional connections and considering how to do so. People often talk about change, but do not actively experiment with changes in personal behavior.
Level 3	Preparation	Compelled to change behavior and creating specific plans to do so. Focused on solutions.
Level 4	Action	Changing behaviors, concepts of self, and conceptions of self relative to others. Taking action and willingly engaging others.
Level 5	Maintenance	Maintaining emotional connections through thoughtful and intentional action. Continuing efforts toward creating emotional connections.

Consider the level you currently fit in. What would you need to change to reach level four—Action?

The five stages of change include: precontemplation, contemplation, preparation, action, and maintenance.

- During the precontemplation stage, individuals don't intend to change because they are unaware or under-informed about the need to change, or they unsuccessfully tried to change once and became demoralized.
- During the contemplation stage, individuals intend to change, but are somewhat ambivalent because they are aware of both the pros and cons to changing.
- During the preparation stage, individuals are ready to change in the immediate future, and have plans to take actions toward that change.
- During the action stage, individuals have made specific, overt changes and work hard to prevent relapse.
- During the maintenance stage, enough time has passed that individuals don't have to work as hard to prevent a relapse and their confidence grows.

The Transtheoretical Model for Change has been applied to a wide variety of problem behaviors,[3] and is an interesting tool to consider when learning how to change to develop emotional connections with others.

Engaging leaders must work to develop emotional connections with others; they must take action to do so. Developing emotional connections can take a lifetime, but the rewards—especially in terms of engagement—are significant.

Engaging leaders recognize a distinction between thoughts and feelings, and they express both to those around them in appropriate

■ ■ ■ ■ ■   **EXERCISE**
Self-Assessment of Emotional Tone

This self-assessment can help you evaluate the emotional tone you set as a leader. There are no right or wrong answers to any of the questions; the aim, rather, is to provide information about the emotional tone you set in the workplace.

Take a few moments to consider each question before responding. Rate yourself by marking responses to each question on the continuum. Of course, genuine honesty and self-reflection during this assessment will provide greater opportunities for you to learn. After you respond to each question by placing your answer on the continuum, reflect on the questions at the end of the exercise.

What kind of emotional tone do you set for the people you lead?

●——●

Emotionally draining   *Positively inspiring*

Do you take action when you witness the emotions of others, or do you try to avoid such situations?

●——●

Avoid   *Recognize*

Are you in touch with the emotional sides of others?

●——●

No/Rarely   *Yes/Often*

How do individuals working around you feel about their work?

●——●

Do not enjoy/Are unhappy   *Do enjoy/Are happy*

How much time have you spent this month asking others how they feel about their work?

●——●

No time   *On a weekly basis*

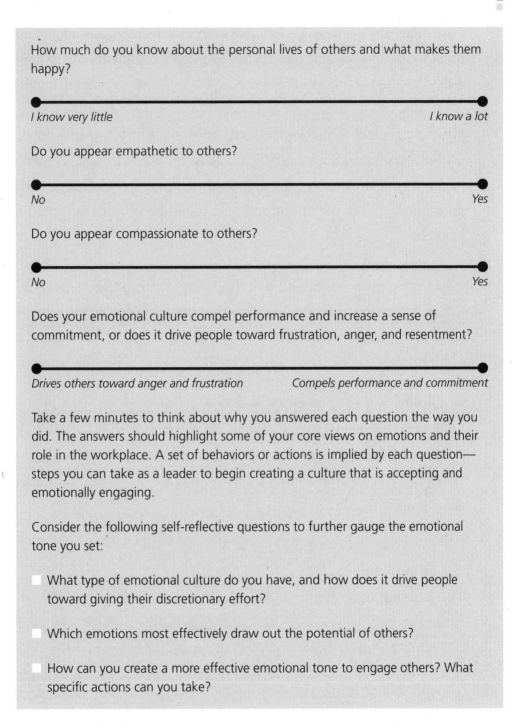

How much do you know about the personal lives of others and what makes them happy?

I know very little   *I know a lot*

Do you appear empathetic to others?

No   *Yes*

Do you appear compassionate to others?

No   *Yes*

Does your emotional culture compel performance and increase a sense of commitment, or does it drive people toward frustration, anger, and resentment?

Drives others toward anger and frustration   *Compels performance and commitment*

Take a few minutes to think about why you answered each question the way you did. The answers should highlight some of your core views on emotions and their role in the workplace. A set of behaviors or actions is implied by each question— steps you can take as a leader to begin creating a culture that is accepting and emotionally engaging.

Consider the following self-reflective questions to further gauge the emotional tone you set:

- What type of emotional culture do you have, and how does it drive people toward giving their discretionary effort?

- Which emotions most effectively draw out the potential of others?

- How can you create a more effective emotional tone to engage others? What specific actions can you take?

ways. They take time to understand their own feelings, homing in on unmet emotional needs and taking responsibility for them through self-motivated action.

Engaging leaders transform frustration or anger into positive energy, releasing emotional debts held against others in order to move forward. And they accept the emotions of others, empathizing with their unmet needs and taking action to meet those needs as much as possible.

All these actions are important for engaging leaders because they lead to more effective management of both personal needs and the needs of others.

Setting an Engaging Emotional Tone

Leaders are the primary role models for others and should therefore be aware of the emotional tone they set for others. They should consider their role in establishing a positive emotional tone in the work environment.

Taking Action

The engaging leader approach begins with the self-mindfulness of leaders and the work they do to understand themselves better. The next step requires interacting with others to engage them emotionally.

Individuals are emotional before they are rational, and they are often deeply emotional beings. These emotions may be hidden or buried because the organizational culture discourages emotions in the workplace. Engaging leaders are not required to dig into the deepest—and sometimes darkest—emotional places of others, but they do need to demonstrate diligence in working to create a comfortable, emotionally engaging environment for those around them.

■ ■ ■ ■ ■ ■ ■ ■ ▪ ▪

"Nothing is so contagious as enthusiasm."

— SAMUEL TAYLOR COLERIDGE, POET AND PHILOSOPHER

▪ ▪ ▪ ▪ ▪ ▪ ▪ ■ ■ ■

One way engaging leaders invite emotions as part of the work culture is by encouraging others to share their feelings. Individual comfort levels and willingness to share vary, but often develop over time. Figure 5-1 offers information about initiating emotional engagement. The left column describes a key action or behavior, the middle column lists associated behavior-focused principles, and the right column offers examples of the principle in action as it might play in random situations.

■ ■ ■ Rekindling a Smoldering Flame

Leaders sometimes encounter individuals who are emotionally nonengaged. Their emotional fatigue often causes them to float through work or simply hang on. Where, how, and why do they lose their energy? And how can emotional engagement rekindle that smoldering flame?

FIGURE 5-1 Emotional Engagement in Action

Action	Principle	Principle in Action
Listen before speaking.	Listen for signals that reveal what is happening below the surface of individuals. Watch for body language and listen for vocal tone.	Someone may share their frustration with a new policy. Introducing a new policy itself is probably not that upsetting, because policies in general are so prevalent in typical work life. Instead, there may be some specific aspect about the policy that is upsetting. A time-keeping policy, for example, may seem like micro-management and it may suggest a lack of trust. The policy itself is not upsetting, but the primary feeling it induces—distrust—is upsetting.
Validate the feelings of others.	Show empathy, understanding, and acceptance. Do not hide, mitigate, or change conversations about emotions. Individuals should feel comfortable discussing emotions in the workplace.	Someone walking out of a meeting appears frustrated or upset. Instead of ignoring them or allowing them to deal with it on their own, an engaging leader would walk up to the person and try to understand their feelings by asking an open-ended question like, "How are you doing today?" The response may be a simple "ok," but it may also reveal their frustrations. Let them know it is all right to feel frustrated and that you want to understand why they are frustrated. Give them a comfortable environment to discuss their feelings.
Do not label others.	Try to understand individuals on a situation-by-situation basis. Labeling others confines them to the label, and it will be very difficult to view them any other way moving forward. Instead, identify their emotions in the given situation. Treat every situation as unique and different.	A young woman who got upset and began crying on one occasion was labeled a crier. The label carries a lot of weight in how others interact with her now. It essentially supports an inference in a way that has a negative effect on her relationships. Instead of labeling her, look to understand her emotions in the situation when she first cried. An engaging leader should take the opportunity to engage her emotionally and look for ways to support her.

Action	Principle	Principle in Action
Monitor your ladder of inference.	When you may be judging someone, check your ladder of inference. Try to simply listen and be non-judgmental until it becomes possible to inquire further and work to really understand a situation. First note your own reactions, then begin analyzing the situation.	A very loud, vocal person asserts himself every time he feels challenged. Noticing his defensiveness, you begin to think he is insecure and he speaks loudly to avoid challenges. Instead of perpetuating your inferences and allowing them shape subsequent actions, you stop to consider whether it is true that everyone who speaks loudly is necessarily insecure. Realizing this is not necessarily true, you decide that you will treat him as an individual and speak to him directly.
Express yourself.	A great way to emotionally engage others is to express your own emotions in an appropriate manner.	You feel nervous about an upcoming decision by the executive director because it may delegate a significant amount of additional work to your team. Instead of suppressing that nervousness, share your thoughts with others by saying, "Waiting for this decision makes me nervous. I know it's an exciting opportunity for us, but I feel the extra responsibility will also be very challenging."
Ask others to express themselves.	Asking others how they feel is the most direct way to elicit their emotions. Explicit conversations prevent guessing about their emotions and ways to engage them. They allow more compassionate connections, and they provide opportunities to leverage emotions productively.	Your team is feeling a tremendous amount of stress due to a high volume of work. Instead of accepting the stress as an inevitable part of business, ask your team members how they are feeling. You can work together to find solutions, helping them manage their workload as efficiently as possible to regain a sense of control.

Action	Principle	Principle in Action
Balance care with progress.	This demonstrates your care, understanding, and respect, but does so in a way that supports both the individual and progress. Demonstrate care for the individual. Once you understand the individual's emotions, inquire about its relation to work and making progress.	Joe is a curt guy who rarely shows emotions. Lately he has seemed especially overwhelmed. Instead of forcing him to share his feelings, simply demonstrate your care for him by saying, "Joe, I sense that you may be feeling overwhelmed. My perception may or may not be accurate, and I do not want to intrude into your personal space. However, I want you to know if there is anything I can do to support you or help you, please do not hesitate to ask. Also, if there is anything I can do to help support you in your work, please let me know."

The following example highlights how an individual can become emotionally non-engaged.

> Meghan worked extremely hard to revamp the customer inquiry process. She met with other managers, reviewed customer satisfaction data, and analyzed the process. The experience came with many ups and downs, especially because she met many others who were unhappy about the impending changes. They were skeptical and did not want to change their old ways, despite their customers' frequent dissatisfaction.
>
> After finally implementing the new process, Meghan became upset. Her supervisor failed to acknowledge her hard work. He had monitored her tasks, but otherwise seemed to care little about the emotional strain it cost to be surrounded by such

contention and negativity throughout the project. In fact, he even nonchalantly suggested that she begin revamping other processes.

Because she does not want to upset her supervisor, Meghan agrees to begin the new project. But she feels terribly unappreciated, and the feeling wears at her as she begins her next assignment. Pretty soon thereafter, her once-positive attitude about revamping the team processes changes. Meghan begins transitioning from a actively engaged person to a non-engaged person. Her attitude changes, as do her levels of commitment and passion toward her assignment.

■ ■ ■ ■ ■ ■ **PRINCIPLE**

Non-engagement is often an expression of unmet emotional needs.

Engaging leaders can help emotionally reengage individuals like Meghan by helping them reconnect to what makes them feel excited or passionate about their work. Most individuals become non-engaged because they have unmet emotional needs. Leaders must discover, through questions and discussion, what emotional need is unmet and take action toward reengaging the individual. In Meghan's situation, her unmet emotional need was recognition.

■ ■ ■ ■ ■ ■ ■ ■ ■

"Enthusiasts at work. Cynics Keep Out."

— TOM PETERS, AUTHOR AND BUSINESS MANAGEMENT CONSULTANT

Most people have probably worked with an individual like Meghan, or have gone through a similar experience themselves. Because her need to feel appreciated is unmet, her engagement levels change in a negative way. If her supervisor had given more attention to her feelings and demonstrated his appreciation, she most likely would have tackled her next assignment with the same vigor and the same level of engagement as her first assignment. Engaging leaders are aware of individuals like Meghan and they find ways to help them reconnect emotionally to their work.

Leaders should never ignore the role emotions play in individual engagement. They should work to find ways of connecting with and leveraging individual emotions. Doing so will increase shared understanding, trust, commitment, and performance.

A Story about Using Emotions to Counter Active Disengagement

In 1914, Sir Ernest Shackleton led a British Antarctic expedition. His ship, *Endurance*, became trapped and eventually crushed by ice early in the expedition. Abandoning the ship, his crew was starving, frightened, and wanted to give up. But he refused to allow his crew to disengage. Having been able to salvage three small boats, his team fled to a nearby island and camped on the ice for nearly five months. He used positive emotions to counter their active disengagement. After 600 days and by using a small boat to traverse 800 treacherous miles, he was able to guide his crew to a remote whaling station, where he organized their eventual rescue. Leveraging his positive emotions to prevent his crew from allowing their negative emotions to take over, he saved every man's life.

ENDNOTES

1. The Corporate Leadership Council, *Engaging the Workforce: Focusing on Critical Leverage Points to Drive Employee Engagement* (Washington, D.C.: The Corporate Executive Board, 2004).

2. J. O. Prochaska and C. C. DiClemente. "Stages and Processes of Self-Change of Smoking: Toward an Integrative Model of Change," *Journal of Consulting and Clinical Psychology*, 51(3): 390-395, 1983. A detailed overview of the Transtheoretical Model of Change is available online at http://www.uri.edu/research/cprc/TTM/detailedoverview.htm (accessed August 2007).

3. Ibid.

RECOMMENDED READING

Boyatzis, Richard E., Daniel Goleman, Ph.D., and Annie McKee. *Primal Leadership: Realizing the Power of Emotional Intelligence.* Boston: Harvard Business School Press, 2002.

Goleman, Daniel, Ph.D. *Emotional Intelligence: Why It Can Matter More Than IQ.* New York: Bantam Books, 1997.

Goleman, Daniel, Ph.D. "What Makes a Leader?" *Harvard Business Review* Nov.-Dec., 1998. Boston: Harvard Business School Press.

Hughes, Marcia, Bonita L. Patterson, and James B. Terrell. *Emotional Intelligence in Action: Training and Coaching Activities for Leaders and Managers.* San Francisco: Pfeiffer, 2005.

6 A Holistic Approach to Engaging Leadership

Leaders must consider their perceptions of strong leadership in the context of today's modern workforce. They will probably find it necessary to reframe the tenets of traditional, command- and task-oriented leadership to embrace instead a new, engaging approach to leadership. Engaging leadership focuses on personal respect for others and aims to work with individuals to harness their energy and potential in ways that meet overarching organizational goals. To earn the commitment of engaged individuals, engaging leaders should be accessible and humble through self-disclosure, self-awareness, and meaningful, honest discussion.

It is important to think of individuals holistically. To foster engagement, leaders must remember that the principles espoused by the

four cornerstones extend beyond the individual as a knowledge work-
er to the personal life and composition of the individual as a whole.
Individuals who are healthy and happy at work are more likely to be
healthy and happy in their personal lives as well, and vice versa. Holistic engagement maximizes individual potential.

Like trust, engaging environments take a long time to build and just
moments to destroy, and not everyone can completely engage all the
time. Individual engagement levels naturally ebb and flow. It is very
difficult to change a culture of widespread disengagement, and actively disengaged individuals are never transformed overnight. Engaging leaders should focus most of their energy on the segments of
the workforce with the greatest potential to engage and contribute:
actively engaged and non-engaged individuals. Set realistic expectations, and keep in mind that every interactive moment provides an
opportunity to engage others.

■ ■ ■ Applying the Engaging Leader Approach to Unique Individuals

Engaging leaders must recognize the uniqueness of each individual,
determining what they want and need to maximize their potential.
Develop interpersonal relationships using the four cornerstones of
engaging leadership: (1) build trust as the foundation of effective relationships; (2) motivate individuals in ways that are uniquely meaningful to them; (3) take a people-centric approach to managing performance; and (4) engage the emotions of others in their work.

■ ■ ■ Interrelationships among the Cornerstones

The cornerstones of engaging leadership interrelate and build off each
other. Leaders must balance these cornerstones and their interrela-

tionships by applying their principles according to individual needs and greater organizational contexts.

An analogy given earlier describes how the meaning of engaging leadership varies among individuals like nutritional needs vary among individuals. Individuals want and need different portions and types of nourishment, at different times and in different ways. Some prefer small bites of a variety of foods, while others prefer large portions of a single food. Some prefer fruit for breakfast, while others never have an appetite before lunch.

In the same way, one individual may need to develop a deeper sense of trust before discussing personal motivations, while another may divulge motivations without requiring as much trust. One individual may need a detailed description of the relationship between his or her work and the greater goals of the organization, while another may naturally equate the two.

Building trust with and among others is not only a fundamental cornerstone of engaging leadership itself, but it is also necessary to engage individuals with the principles espoused by every other cornerstone. Leaders must facilitate trust through open, honest, and direct communications to leverage and enhance the motivation, performance, and emotions of others. Individuals who lack trust in a relationship with their leader, for example, are much less likely to share personal motivations, which can diminish opportunities for engagement.

To give another example of interrelationships among the cornerstones: Understanding individual motivations is the second cornerstone of engaging leadership, but it also facilitates the third cornerstone's premise by promoting a people-centric approach to managing performance.

Understanding an individual's unique motivators arms the leader with the information needed to take a people-centric approach to managing others' performance. Without a solid understanding of a person's unique motivators, the leader is at worst going to operate from a manager-centric approach and at best is likely to make assumptions about a person's motivators.

Knowing what motivates someone puts the leader in a position to create situations that meet the interests, needs, and motivational preferences of an individual. Whether it be delegating specific work assignments or leveraging a person's strengths in a given situation, the leader is in a position to more readily leverage the individual and his or her unique motivators.

Understanding motivations also provides insight into the emotional connections individuals have with their work. This provides leaders an opportunity to enhance those connections, making them more meaningful and facilitating engagement in the process.

On the whole, understanding and employing each of the four cornerstones is critical to being an effective leader in the 21st century. Together they form the engaging leader approach that allows leaders to elicit the best efforts from others.

■ ■ ■ ■ ■ ■ ■ ■ ■ ■

"Change the rules before somebody else does."

— TOM PETERS, *REIMAGINE*

▪ ▪ ▪ Daily Challenges to Engagement

Engaging leaders face challenges on a daily basis. But, as Woody Allen once said, 80 percent of success comes from just showing up. Engaging leaders show up and make engagement a priority in their work strategies. This often means making tradeoffs and shifting paradigms about working relationships. The differences between non-engaged people and actively engaged employees—higher productivity, increased satisfaction, less turnover, and better health, among others—is well worth the effort, though. Leaders can hardly afford to *not* make engaging leadership a priority.

▪ ▪ Time Constraints

Initially, engaging leadership may take up a significant amount of time and effort. Leaders may need take time to consider their current leadership approach and its implications, formulating future plans to help engage others. But over time and with practice, the engaging leader approach becomes more comfortable and natural, and leaders will spend more energy maintaining engagement rather than building it.

Leaders can initially invest any level of effort they choose. But, just like in the stock market, greater investment initially leads to increased chances for positive returns later, and those increased returns can then compound to create even greater growth in value. Engaging leaders must commit the time and effort it takes to follow the four cornerstones of engaging leadership if they are going to be successful in maximizing the potential of others and accessing discretionary effort.

■ ■ Active Disengagement

Engaging leaders should be cognizant of the disproportionate amount of time it takes to battle active disengagement. Although the situation is far from hopeless, research suggests that some portion of the workforce will always be actively disengaged, and leaders have to work much harder to transition actively disengaged individuals into non-engaged individuals, a place where they still are not maximizing their potential.

Nevertheless, leaders must not ignore actively disengaged individuals. Their negative behaviors may have an adverse effect on the higher engagement levels of others, which can compromise the entire organization.

Actively disengaged individuals do not respond to the engaging leader approach as other groups do. The key to tackling active disengagement is understanding why these individuals have become so disgruntled and negative in the first place. This requires patience and a willingness to be open-minded and listen, suspend judgment or blame, and accept ownership as the person most able to influence an individual's engagement. Over the course of time, you, as an engaging leader, must work to rebuild trust with the individual. You must show them you genuinely care and then take authentic actions towards reengaging the person.

Placing too much attention on their negativity can backfire, as many actively disengaged individuals believe their ability to exert influence is rooted in their negativity and poor attitudes. Focusing on the negativity can further root those tendencies. Instead, you must start small and focus on rebuilding positive connections with and for the individual.

■ ■ ■ ■ ■   **PRACTICE TOOL**
A Discussion with Actively Disengaged Individuals

While engaging leaders should focus most of their time on fostering the potential of those who are actively engaged or non-engaged, they should not ignore those who are actively disengaged. The following steps, when coupled with tempered expectations, will help you have constructive discussions with actively disengaged individuals.

1. State your assumptions about the individual's active disengagement and explain your reasons by describing particular behaviors.

2. Express your intentions—to help them reengage in their work—and ask for a response to your assessment.

3. Explain that to help them reengage, you will need their help. Ask what you can both do together to help them become more excited and passionate about their work. Individuals respond to this question in countless ways, so be sure to just sit and listen carefully without judging their response.

4. After they respond, paraphrase what you heard to ensure that you share an understanding about what they said, then tell them that you understand.

5. State your commitment to helping them reengage. Begin by discussing the suggestions they made about what was needed to reengage. Make suggestions yourself, as appropriate. Use the four cornerstones of engaging leadership and the lessons of this book as a foundation for the discussion.

6. Commit explicitly to action by describing exactly what each of you will do to help the individual reengage. Ask them to commit to action, too, and agree on ways you both will keep your commitments to one another.

7. Develop plans for communication and action if things get off track. This demonstrates your desire to establish a basis of trust and to commit to positive action.

These small steps can create powerful momentum in the right direction.

Often these individuals do not feel in control of their own lives or destiny. Leaders should resist accepting too much ownership in efforts to reengage them. Instead, make sure they are involved and accept ownership and accountability throughout the process.

And finally, leaders must gauge how quickly they move with actively disengaged individuals. Most actively engaged individuals are capable of spotting disingenuous, untrustworthy, or non-benevolent behaviors right away—perceptions that often manifest themselves in a resurgence of actively disengaged behaviors. Like pulling someone out of quicksand, slow and steady movements are the best approach.

High Turnover Rates

Every organization faces the challenge of fluctuating turnover rates over time. Individuals come and go for myriad reasons, and given today's global market and increased expectations for meaning and fulfillment in work, this trend will likely continue. One way to minimize this trend is by working to maintain high engagement levels. People who are engaged find their work satisfying and challenging, which are key reasons to stay with an organization. Beyond that, people enjoy working for leaders who have their best interests in mind—another reason to stay at an organization.

When engaged individuals do leave organizations, however, actively seek out engaged individuals to replace them. One way to hire engaged people is to recognize what engaged people look like and do in your organization. Being able to have an engaged person to compare a candidate to is a great place to start. In addition, asking interview questions that uncover individual work-related preferences and their suitability in your workplace, including their unique triggers for engagement, can enable a hiring manager to see if he or she can meet and sustain the individuals' needs. Hiring engaged individuals will help minimize the amount of time and energy needed to build and maintain their engagement later.

Shifting Priorities

With the fast pace of today's organizations, a leader's focus may be in a perpetual state of shifting and adjusting priorities. Something *always* takes precedence or priority over something else. On a broader level, new organizational leaders often initiate new goals and strategies that pull leaders in new directions, market changes mean new customer demands, and technology can quickly change everything within the business landscape. On an organizational or team level, staffing levels, waning stakeholder or customer satisfaction, new products or services in the market, or even morale can shift priorities.

One priority that should never change, though, is the proactive work of engaging others. Building and maintaining a workplace where engaged individuals motivate themselves and their teams by using their discretionary effort should always be viewed as a crucial element in achieving organizational goals.

One way to effectively respond to ever-shifting priorities is to recognize that engaged individuals emulate engaged leaders. Engaged workforces do not occur on their own. Engaging leaders throughout the organization must champion engagement by keeping it a priority no matter what.

Another way to keep engagement a constant priority is to remember that engagement occurs one individual at a time. Leaders working diligently to engage each individual will build a solid, engaged workforce. Actively engaged workforces need maintenance, too. Engaging leaders should strategize and think about engagement as a long-term commitment that withstands shifting priorities.

Supervisors Who Do Not Support Engaging Leadership

Some leaders have supportive supervisors who are both engaged themselves and engaging with others, while other leaders may not have this kind of support. The implications are significant because supervisors have the most influence over the engagement levels of those they lead. When their supervisors are not themselves engaged nor engaging others, leaders will have a very difficult time finding opportunities to build trust, effectively manage performance, and leverage unique motivators and emotions.

Of course, leaders can try to manage their own engagement without the support of a supervisor, but it is more difficult to sustain. Another option is to initiate an explicit discussion with your supervisor to specifically articulate and describe your personal needs. It is important to also describe the kind of support needed to achieve certain goals. Relating needs to specific work-related goals adds a meaningful incentive for supervisors to commit to building a more engaged relationship.

Even if your supervisor chooses not to take action after the discussion, you have at least accepted personal responsibility in the situation and have taken steps to change current conditions. Applying the engaging leader approach to a situation provides valuable practice, and in some cases, this may be all you can do for the time being.

Engaging Leadership as Part of a System

Even with an excellent, engaged supervisor, engaging leaders are often part of a leadership system that may or may not be engaging. The best way to demonstrate the value of engaging leadership to others in the system is to believe in and adopt the engaging leader approach yourself, and then present the positive results to everyone.

"You must be the change you wish to see in the world."

— MAHATMA GANDHI, SPIRITUAL LEADER

Parts of the system may not support engaging leadership, including an organization's culture, its specific processes and procedures, performance management systems, compensation systems, or even the workforce itself. While these factors may limit their scope of influence, engaged leaders should focus on the parts they can control. In any context, it is possible to interact with others and leverage their influence to effect positive change. Engaging leaders will produce results and meet organizational goals, which often proves to be a principal impetus behind system changes.

When engaging leaders build trust across a system, it creates opportunities for a variety of stakeholders to leverage their strengths and produce results, which they can then share with other parts of the system. Engaging leaders offer positive recognition to other engaged individuals and openly discuss the importance and value of engaging leadership. These actions may not change the system immediately or holistically, but their ripple effect will be positive.

Sustaining Engaging Leadership over Time

Sustaining engagement can be draining, and it is difficult for anyone to remain engaged 100 percent of the time, which is why it is important to consider engagement from a perspective of consistency over time. Leaders should focus their efforts realistically, but they should also aim to create conditions for sustained, engaging work environments.

PRACTICE TOOL
Sustaining Engaging Leadership over Time

Use the following tips as tools to help sustain engagement over time:

- Gauge the readiness of the individuals you want to engage. The change-readiness model introduced in Chapter 5 shows that different individuals are not all ready for engagement in the same way or at the same time. Take some time to assess individual readiness levels one at a time, and factor those levels into your engagement approach.

- Take small steps, and set small milestones for getting to know individuals personally. By getting to know others in small steps over time, engaging leaders can make inroads toward meaningful relationships built on trust.

- Take action toward working in a different way. Just reading about engagement may be a big first step. Instead of changing your entire approach all at once, begin by trying to incorporate certain techniques of the engaging leader approach one at a time.

- Discuss engaging leadership with others, including your supervisor. Establish ways to apply the approach when possible, like simply using a few of the recommended conversational starters, for example.

- Ask for feedback. Feedback is nourishment. Engaging leaders must receive feedback—in addition to providing it to others. This may mean explicitly asking colleagues and supervisors to provide feedback.

When done deliberately and well, engaging others is contagious. Engaged individuals will begin to role-model the behaviors their leaders demonstrate, ultimately creating a culture of engagement.

Continued Self-Engagement

Not only do leaders have a responsibility to influence the engagement levels of others, but they are also responsible for monitoring and maintaining their own levels of engagement. Given their ability to "thin-slice" others and situations, people will recognize leaders who are non-engaged. While leaders may want to focus their attention on others' engagement rather than their own, it sends the wrong message to ask others to engage if leaders are not trying to do the same themselves.

As the primary role model for others, leaders need to be adept at monitoring their own engagement. This requires emotional self-awareness, and it means initiating conversations with their own supervisors about trust, motivation, and performance. By actively monitoring and managing their own level of engagement, leaders can help themselves thrive while also helping others.

Be Resilient

Engaging leadership requires a deep sense of commitment and a willingness to engage. Engaging leaders will often face unplanned-for situations and disappointment. Their team members may not always shine, nor will they always provide the support leaders need. Leaders themselves may at times want to disengage. Resilience plays a large role in sustaining engagement over time.

Just as individual needs and preferences vary with regard to engagement, leaders themselves will have individual methods of resilience. Some universal tips on resilience can be applied in individual ways as appropriate: align personal values with your work as a leader, leverage your own strengths and enjoyments, and be more flexible.

Most individuals feel energized by their personal values. Engaging leaders value a people-centric leadership approach that utilizes the talents and strengths of others to accomplish outstanding results. Some values associated with this type of approach include integrity, directness, honesty, empathy, and individualized attention. It is important for engaging leaders to explore what engagement means to them and how it aligns with their personal values. Achieving an alignment between their leadership approach and their personal values will help minimize the stress and challenges associated with engaging leadership, and it will increase their individual resiliency.

▪ ▪ ▪ ▪ ▪ ▪ PRINCIPLE

Maintain resiliency by aligning your values and aspirations with personal strengths.

Another way engaging leaders can maintain personal resilience is by developing and using their own strengths. Revisiting individual strengths with a supervisor, mentor, or coach often reminds leaders of their contributions, creating feelings of empowerment and energy. It usually also helps focus that energy on aspects of work they enjoy.

Being more flexible in various aspects of work and life can also increase resilience. Maintaining rigidness and resisting change take a tremendous amount of time and energy. By developing flexibility, accepting change, and keeping things in perspective (with a positive outlook), leaders can bounce back from adversity more quickly. Taking care of yourself by being active, eating healthily, and sleeping well also helps.

"If your actions inspire others to dream more, learn more, do more, and become more, you are a leader."

— JOHN QUINCY ADAMS, U.S. PRESIDENT

Start Today

Today is the best day to begin practicing the engaging leader approach. Let yourself dream about what you can accomplish (see introductory exercise, *Dreaming Big to Unleash the Potential of Others*). Engaging leaders engage themselves and take action. They hold themselves accountable for connecting and cooperating with others, making that cooperation greater than their own status as leaders. They appreciate their own talents, strengths, and contributions, and they recognize the holistic nature of people. Engaging leaders tap into the potential of others in a way that allows everyone—and the greater organization itself—to succeed.

PRINCIPLE

Make your cooperation greater than your individual status.

Principles of Engaging Leadership

- In the 21st century's global market, leaders cannot depend on only currently engaged individuals to produce successful results. It is necessary to increase engagement from others, too.

- Engaging leaders resolve to not let individuals disengage, but instead, proactively work to engage others.

- Engaging leaders believe in people. It is people and their use of discretionary effort that differentiate high-performing organizations from the rest.

- A strong interpersonal connection with a leader is the primer for individual engagement.

- To be authentic and genuine, you must understand who you are (and who you are not) and who you want to be as a leader.

- Trust is the foundation of engaging leadership.

- In the 21st century workforce, benevolence has the greatest influence on trust in relationships between leaders and others.

- Building a trusting relationship requires authenticity.

- A sense of pride, ownership, and passion for your work are the key intrinsic motivators.

- Engaging leaders help others accept ownership and responsibility for motivating themselves.

- People do not change easily. Get to know them as the individuals they are, not as you want them to be.

- Do not make assumptions about individual motivators. Instead, have explicit conversations with others about their motivation.

- Every interaction is an opportunity to better understand others' unique motivators.

- Demonstrating empathy while managing performance is the first step to a more people-centric approach.

- Engaging leaders find ways to intentionally involve people in decisions that affect them.

- For maximum engagement, individuals must be held accountable for their work. Accountability demonstrates that an individual's work is important.

- Engaging leaders systematically and consistently find ways to tap into individual strengths.

- Even though our work lives go by in days, weeks, and months, we really live for moments of contribution, value, and personal pride and fulfillment. Consistent recognition is a primer for engagement.

- Individuals are emotional before they are rational, and emotions drive engagement.

- We cannot separate who we are in life from who we are at work. Whole people needed to be treated like whole people, which includes their emotional self.

- Non-engagement is often an expression of unmet emotional needs.

- Maintain resiliency by aligning your values and aspirations with personal strengths.

- Make your cooperation greater than your individual status.

■ ■ ■ ■ ■   **EXERCISE**
What Will Your Story Be?

I hope you feel compelled to take action toward becoming a more engaging leader. In the exercise in the Introduction, you considered what *could* happen through engaging leadership. Now it is up to you to write the story of what *will* happen. What will you accomplish as an engaging leader?

To help you get started, take a moment to write a personal letter of intent for different periods of time as they elapse (30 days, six months, and one year). Describe what you hope to accomplish and what you can do to ensure it happens.

30 Days from Today

Six Months from Today

One Year From Today

Best of luck in your quest to become an engaging leader! And remember to always strive to find the best in yourself and in others.

RECOMMENDED READING

Stoltz, Paul G. *Adversity Quotient at Work: Finding Your Hidden Capacity for Getting Things Done.* New York: Harper Collins Publishers, 2000.

A Perspective on Engagement
(Four Months Later)

Dear Leader,

A few months have gone by since I wrote my last letter. At the time, I was feeling sapped of energy and passion for my work. I had come to the position really hoping to contribute and succeed, but after only a short period, I felt disenfranchised and wrote to you about it. I am glad to tell you that things have changed and I am feeling much more positive at work. The noticeable changes in my supervisor's leadership behaviors have really made a difference.

My manager began trusting others to work on important assignments, instead of taking care of them all himself. In fact, I've had a chance to work on several significant assignments in the past few months, more than in my entire first two years! This has been extremely exciting for me. He is also talking more openly about trusting my teammates and me, and it feels good. It actually makes me trust him more, too.

When he delegates assignments, he explains their importance and points out how they contribute to greater organizational goals. These discussions have been especially energizing because I never really knew much about our organization's goals, but now I do and I feel good about my contributions. And it's nice to know he cares about both me and the organization.

I've noticed his efforts to inquire more about what I want to accomplish and why. We've had discussions about what motivates me and what I feel passionate about. He says he wants to create more opportunities to help my work connect more closely with my interests, motivations, and passions.

I really feel much more connected to my job and to my supervisor. I had almost given up hope and began looking for another job. Now I am feeling rejuvenated and am committed to giving my best efforts toward the work we do here. With his new leadership approach, my supervisor has made me really believe I can make a difference in this organization and be personally happy as well.

I am feeling more and more engaged in my work every day.

> *Sincerely,*
> *Actively Engaged at Work*

Index